Glass
A Portrait

Printed in the United Kingdom by Biddles Ltd, Surrey

Published by Sanctuary Publishing Limited, Sanctuary House, 45–53 Sinclair Road,
London W14 0NS, United Kingdom

www.sanctuarypublishing.com

ISBN: 1-86074-347-1

Glass
A Portrait

Robert Maycock

Sanctuary

About The Author

Robert Maycock is one of the leading writers on music in Britain, covering a range from classical through contemporary to world music. He has been editor of the magazine *Classical Music* and the music pages of the *Independent* national newspaper. *Classic FM* magazine, in its first issue, named him as one of three British opera critics worth reading.

In both writing and editing he has worked to develop the scope of the music press, so that it better reflects the realities of the music business and of the worldwide diversity of styles, forms and musically active cultures. He is a long-standing adviser to the Arts Council and the UK funding system, and has written major documents for them on national arts and music policy.

Starting professional life on the staff of the science journal *Nature* – he studied the history and philosophy of science as well as music – he has also programmed festivals and set up a travel company, and is currently a director of the cross-cultural music group ShivaNova along with his partner, the composer/performer Priti Paintal. Their family live as near as possible to France and they visit India whenever they can.

Contents

Prologue

What were you doing when you first heard music by Philip Glass? This is not an impertinent question. For most people the answer is going to be anything other than sitting in a concert hall or playing a CD. But the real reason for asking is that most people tend to remember. This is a singular position for a contemporary classical composer. During most of the half century of his creative life up to now, listeners in this field have come to expect bad experiences, which they soon block out and make up their minds to avoid in the future. Only in the last decade has the situation improved, and even then only for a minority of mainstream classical audiences and a minority of composers.

In the case of Glass, even though he is a leading member of this composers' minority, it was always different. Once he was past his student days, people first heard his music in Paris fringe theatres or Manhattan studios and galleries. Then it turned up in European drama festivals. The same show bewildered and stunned its audiences at the Metropolitan Opera House in New York, but it played there outside the main season and drew a different public. This was enough to start a long career of composing operas, though even now they are likely to appear in less conventional opera venues: the European première of his 2002 opera *Galileo Galilei* was booked not for the Paris Opera or Covent Garden but for the Barbican Theatre, London, part of a multi-art-form centre. In Britain, Covent Garden has never staged his works, nor have the other established companies, apart from English National Opera, which put on two during a short-lived radical period the company went through in the 1980s.

Millions will have heard his film scores, whether they knew it or not. If you went to see *The Truman Show* a second time, you would have recognized the soundtrack even if you could not put a name to it. Some have set out to listen to his *Low* and *Heroes* symphonies thinking they might be arrangements of David Bowie and were often bewildered, but sometimes drawn in, because, while the symphonies use themes drawn from Bowie and Brian Eno as starting points, the music is very much Glass's own. The Philip Glass Ensemble toured and the recordings started to build up. When they were broadcast you would hear them on jazz or cult stations, even cultural review programmes, rather than the traditional classical networks. The Kronos Quartet has championed his music for their own medium and brought it to new listeners. Since the 1990s Glass has written a substantial body of orchestral and concert music, which you are still more likely to hear playing in record shops than over the air. It all adds up. You know it when you hear it. Composers for television and advertising imitate his music and you immediately understand what they have modelled their efforts on. Whatever the means by which you first came by Glass's music, you remember it.

That is because you either love the music or hate it. The repetitions make you ecstatic or they drive you mad. Because the first thing Glass did to make his mark on the world was to use a degree of repetition that was quite unprecedented in Western classical music until a handful of American composers started, in their various ways, to explore its possibilities. In his music from the late 1960s, short phrases turn over again and again, expanding and developing and interacting with others, but always remaining recognizable. Even now, although the numbers of layers in his music and the sophistication of its forms have changed radically, something is always in there repeating itself, whether it is a basic rhythm or a little arpeggio or a huge block of musical elements. The repeats are simply a consequence of Glass's way of building up large-scale forms, not an end in themselves, but they are what you hear on the surface and they are the cause of the initial, unforgettable gut reaction.

Unforgettable but capable of change: this is the article of faith on which this book rests. For it is written by somebody who spent several years taking great care to avoid Glass's music altogether. Vigorous resistance means that the object of disaffection is powerful enough to generate strong feelings. The real poison is indifference. My misfortune was to come across repetitive music through its offshoots among the English experimental composers who used to play the university scene in the 1970s. They, rather than any of the American composers, were the cue for my irrational rage and unrestrained loathing but it was enough for me to keep my ears closed to all such music. An education as a student of contemporary music had been sufficient, as in so many cases, to instil in me the belief that the true path was to be found in the heavyweight European figures of Luciano Berio, Pierre Boulez, Gyorgy Ligeti and Karlheinz Stockhausen, and the messier English generation of Harrison Birtwistle and Peter Maxwell Davies. Studying with Alexander Goehr, a respected colleague and contemporary of the latter two, who possesses an unequalled knowledge, skill and persuasive power in the line of 20th-century music that descended from Arnold Schoenberg, only strengthened this attitude. It took some convincing conversations of quite unreasonable patience on the part of fellow postgraduate, Keith Potter (who was to pioneer an admired trail as one of the first academic specialists in minimal music), before the thought of deliberately listening to one of the new American composers became possible without a red mist forming. Ironically the moment of truth was a tour by Steve Reich And Musicians in which they played the classic *Drumming* and the then new *Music For 18 Musicians* at the Round House in London. At the time it was just an overwhelming one-off experience and did not change my musical world-view, but it proved to be the earthquake that caused cracks in the foundations of my deeply settled prejudice about contemporary music. The prejudice slowly subsided over the coming years until a more inclusive and understanding mind-set could take its place.

I was well prepared for my first experience of the Philip Glass Ensemble and it left an indelible mark on me. It was a tour to promote their latest album. The record, *Glassworks*, was a user-friendly package designed to make the sound and aesthetic of Glass's major works of the late 1970s accessible, through a sequence of shorter pieces, to audiences that might not have had the chance or inclination to attend very long performances. In London the venue was the Sadler's Wells Theatre, usually the host of dance and lyric theatre. For Glass, it was a typical choice away from the halls most associated with classical concert music and its customary audiences. The place was packed with a very mixed audience, which included a wide age range though it looked to contain more young people than most concerts I was used to covering (at the time I was editor of *Classical Music* magazine). The music was played loud and the amplification level was high, though not so high by rock standards. The performance was ferociously concentrated and physical, but the musicians' actions were quite unlike those of a pop concert because the body movement was a necessary means of keeping players together and giving cues at constant high speed.

In the theatre the atmosphere became hot both literally and emotionally. It was unlike any other experience of Western music – I hadn't yet been to an African concert – in that it had the abandon of a rock festival, the precision and intellect of classical traditions and a passionate spirituality that was entirely its own. Through the energy and drive came a huge, joyous confidence and an unexpected inner stillness. I was hooked. I was also, as far as my own profession was concerned, more or less on my own. The critical establishment had turned out in force, mostly wearing the expressionless gaze of those who know in advance that something is going to be bad. You could sense the pleasantly masochistic anticipation of the chance to send in a scathing review. As the evening went on, the gazes turned into steady frowns and, in one or two cases, an outright glare. A treasured memory is of the late Peter Heyworth, critic of *The Observer* and a combative champion of all things modernist, stomping out well before the end in a fury of high-camp exasperation such as only he among his peers could summon up.

From then on it became a matter of enormous curiosity and pleasure to follow the progress of this unique and, as it turns out, uniquely influential figure. The journey was full of surprises. Of the composers who came to maturity in the age of minimalism, Glass has developed more than any, while remaining to some extent an outsider to mainstream traditions. When the critics belatedly came to accept what the age was actually on about their preferred composer was Steve Reich, who had been taken on by a standard publisher and appeared to share many of the modernist ideals. This is despite the growing sense that his later music sounds limited by its lack of expressive range – the genuinely affecting nature of many of his works when performed live comes from their non-musical elements, such as recorded voices or film clips – and ill at ease with larger musical line-ups such as orchestras. John Adams also has a critical following, though his virtuoso range of styles and genres really marks him out as belonging to the next generation, which built on the achievements of the pioneers.

Glass, on the other hand, still gets a bad press, at least from the classical music world. Specialists in other art forms, even other areas of music, and broader-minded cultural commentators, find him an enthralling figure, perhaps because they do not come encumbered by the critical baggage that the classical profession attracts. Even among musicians, a relatively small number (chief among them the conductor

Dennis Russell Davies and the Kronos Quartet) have been responsible for a disproportionate share of commissions, performances and recordings. His success across a wide range of genres, or even his sheer productivity and willingness to accept commissions, has evidently bred suspicion among those who believe, or used to believe, that making deals and running your own business affairs mean selling out. Or perhaps it is just stubborn conservatism that is being reluctantly eroded 20 years after the event, since the voices that used to speak out against Glass the minimalist have been followed by strangely similar voices that now use the austerity of his early work as a stick with which to beat the free and frank expression of Glass today.

Yet look at what, in musical terms, the surprises were. First was his rapid development as an opera composer – something he himself never even thought about until the hit scored by his first big stage collaboration with Robert Wilson (which was not actually conceived as an opera in the customary sense at all) led to a string of invitations from opera houses to write for them. Then, the operas themselves refreshed the genre: in their content, beginning with the trilogy of historical portraits and frequently returning to heroic or quasi-mythic figures such as Columbus and Galileo; in their collaborative working methods and in their impact, which has made nothing less than a massive contribution to keeping contemporary work alive in houses that relied on a settled repertoire with very rare, usually unpopular and rarely revived, new works by the sacred monsters of the composing world.

Glass's early music meanwhile became a huge influence, not only on the post-minimalist generation of classical composers such as John Adams but on commercial composers who found some of its mannerisms easy to imitate, and also on the early days of ambient and dance music as well as the thinking end of pop (Glass was well aware that in choosing Bowie and Eno as inspirations for symphonies, he was returning a compliment). Everybody who goes clubbing is forcibly reminded of this, as looping samples *à la* Reich work their way through Glass-like rhythmic cycles. The outcome is nothing less than a change in the soundscape of Western life, from university music departments, where you can study minimalism as part of music history, to the changing styles of classical commissions and competition entries, to the evolution of pop and to the ambient tapes used to soothe and sell. Even as these currents flowed in their own directions, Glass himself was busy doing other things – film scores, concert music – usually because he was asked to, but in the process he took his language off in new directions filled with burgeoning, romantic melody and an ever wider harmonic spectrum.

It is a well documented career on a day-to-day basis, and strangely short of reflective utterances about the music of recent years except when the composer himself talks about it. Perhaps there just has not been time for anybody to keep up. When Jeff Hudson, then editor at Sanctuary Publishing, proposed a book about Glass while leaving the brief completely open, the direction to take more or less suggested itself. It was time to bring the story up to date, to introduce the composer and his music to anybody looking for a guide and to make the case for Philip Glass as he is now.

Galileo Galilei, Philip Glass's main opera project of 2002, has the unusual quality of telling its story backwards. It places the key events of Galileo's life towards the beginning of its dramatic sequence, and ends up with the great scientist as a boy first looking at the stars. So too this book, which went into production at the same time. Built on interviews with the composer and experience of the music, it focuses at the beginning on the growth areas of the present day and only then turns to what went before. The coincidence is shamelessly opportunistic on the writer's part but, once thought of, it made more and more sense. Much has been written about Glass, but the great bulk of it deals with that mould-breaking period in the 1960s and 1970s when, in the dawning age of American musical minimalism, he started to write music in the way for which he became renowned. There are scholarly studies, specialist books, Keith Potter's epic voyage through the period in *Four Musical Minimalists* and, of course, jokes: 'Knock Knock'/'Who's there?'/'Knock Knock'/'Who's there?'/'Knock Knock'/'Who's there?'/'Philip Glass.'

The joke, with its several variants – making them up is quite easy – shows how far Glass became identified in the public mind with an entire movement. This is not, however, the real truth of the matter, since many composers used more or less minimal styles, from La Monte Young and Terry Riley onwards, while of those who graduated from them, Steve Reich has been arguably almost as influential as Glass. But somehow the notion of a Steve Reich joke doesn't have the same credibility. The popular image of Glass is the composer whose music goes round and round in circles, and it has proved to be a millstone. He is the first to point out that if he ever was a minimalist, he had stopped being one by the time he wrote his most famous early works, *Music In Twelve Parts* for the Philip Glass Ensemble and his first theatre collaboration with Robert Wilson, *Einstein On The Beach*. That was three decades ago.

Also familiar around the world, beginning with the sudden success of *Einstein*, is Philip Glass the opera composer. Many cities and musical centres have seen stagings of his work and many have seen premières, since there are now nearly 20 such pieces of various scales and sizes. Not so many places, however, have seen the production of more than one work, and only a minority of them have been recorded. This state of affairs brings a paradox with it, since Glass himself is in no doubt that theatre and opera work is the core of his life. He has worked in the theatre since he was 20, he developed his personal musical language in the first place to meet the demands and match the aesthetic of the theatre pieces that he was composing for, and he is still driven by ideas for new stage works. Most of his other composing is done because people ask him for it; the operas start from his own mind. Yet almost nobody has seen all his stage works, and few have seen more than a handful. It will take many years' further advance into the age of the DVD and its successors before the nature of Glass as he sees it himself is fully appreciated and experienced even by fans of his music. His own 'professional autobiography', *Music By Philip Glass*, is entirely about stage work apart from its opening and closing sections, although it deals only with the first three operas, the so-called trilogy of portrait operas, *Einstein On The Beach*, *Satyagraha* and *Akhnaten*.

Then there is Philip Glass the film composer. Not only has he collaborated on cult films such as the series of three by Godfrey Reggio that began with *Koyaanisqatsi*, he also wrote a full-length score for Martin Scorsese's portrait of the young Dalai Lama, *Kundun*, and Glass's music was used for the Hollywood hit, *The*

Truman Show. The Hours, due to be released in December 2002, will probably take his music even further afield. With the exception of *Koyaanisqatsi*, which a proportion of the audience went to see for the sake of the music, all this has happened without affecting received notions of Glass's music even though most of the scores are not at all minimal in character, especially since *Kundun*. It is the typical situation with film music: most of the audience has no idea who wrote it, most of the classical music public pays no attention to movie scores and film music buffs only know it in the context of other screen composers.

But what about Philip Glass the writer of symphonic scores? There is next to nothing to read about him. His body of orchestral work seems to have sprung up as though by stealth in the last half decade after only a few earlier pieces, which he started in the late 1980s. Even though it too is nearing 20 major pieces, it is something that he himself considers a sideline. Nevertheless, it is being systematically recorded. All but the last of his six symphonies are internationally available, and while the concertos are lagging behind – a consequence partly of revisions waiting to be made and partly of sheer productivity, since at present they are emerging at about one a year – this is only a matter of time. His first concerto, for violin, has already been taken up by several soloists and has now been recorded three times. What this means is that, in the near future, many more people will be exploring his work initially through the medium of the recordings.

The symphonic work is starting to reach a critical mass at which point it takes on a life of its own, independent of the composer's own perceptions. It is this that decided the back-to-front perspective of the book. What are you most likely to listen to deliberately? Unless you have the resources to jet around, the chance of catching a live performance is relatively rare. It is almost bound to be something on CD. That means the concert music will play a large part. The perspective is different from Glass's own, and in one of the interview sections in this book he talks revealingly about where it may lead, even as he continues to put his prime efforts into seeking out and realizing projects for the stage. There is no question of saying that the composer is right and the public will be wrong, because both perspectives are true. The interaction between them will determine not only how he is considered; but, because he responds positively to commissions, it will also affect what he composes.

All this is for the future. For the present, the book uses the following plan. To begin, and to set the scene, there is an overview of experiencing the music. Listening is futile unless you are on its wavelength. If you get there spontaneously, all well and good, but there is a long history of people wilfully resisting it. It usually helps to accept what the composer actually means, rather than complain that the music doesn't do what you think it ought to. From there, we have a brief taster of work-in-progress – *Galileo Galilei*, only just staged when the book went to press – and then move on to music for orchestra. This and the following chapter about concertos have benefited immeasurably from the opportunity to hear live recordings made at the premières of three recent works: the *Symphony No 6 (Plutonian Ode)*, the *Cello Concerto* and the *Tirol Concerto* for piano and strings. None of these has yet been recorded commercially, and only the *Tirol Concerto* is starting to be performed regularly.

Writing as the first independent person to get to know all three, I have to report that they make a startling extension to the body of Glass's works in two directions: extreme lyrical warmth in the concertos, which are both dominated by long central slow movements, and high emotion in the symphony, which features a solo soprano and is, by some distance, Glass's most powerful concert work to date. As soon as their quality becomes widely known, perhaps by reputation and eventually through recordings, they will be in great demand around the world. They should also be the works that make a decisive difference in the perception of Glass as a concert composer.

Next are theatre, opera and film, and then a chapter that is about Glass's relationship with the world around him, again as it stands now. It explores the way in which he has built up his working practices to use his creative mind to maximum efficiency. Finally, and taking the book's back-to-front movement through time to its logical conclusion, there is a look at the crucial years in the 1960s when all the elements came together and Glass found his true musical voice. Old ground in one sense but, while the information is on the record, no single source contains all of it and each has a different perspective. This is one reason why you still read in potted biographies for concert programmes and the like that he suddenly 'discovered' the rhythms of Indian music and set off in a new direction. Just like that, as though there were nothing more to it.

This chapter contains Glass's most recent pronouncement on the subject. Deliberately, it is as near as the book comes to biography. Even more than with most composers, belying romantic notions of an artist's existence, aside from his family time the life once past its formative years is completely dominated by the work, to the extent that he is often called a workaholic. It is far more rewarding to explore the music, and with time to take one direction or the other – that was the natural way to go.

Throughout the book are extracts from interviews that Glass gave in the spring of 2002 specifically for these purposes – these extracts are indicated by his initials and my questions to him have my initials beside them. To him, then, the primary thanks are due. It turned out to be a period that was busy even by his standards, with *Galileo Galilei, The Hours* and incidental music for a Broadway run of *The Elephant Man* all demanding his creative attention simultaneously as well as the need to get started on a harpsichord concerto. It took some persistence to find the time, but he was resolved to do it and in the end managed it with generosity. The other principal acknowledgment is for unprecedented access to his archives, which included an invaluable range of material from scores, rare photographs through to ephemeral but often revealing articles. Many people at the Looking Glass Studio and Dunvagen, Glass's publishing company, were helpful during my visits to New York, and if I single out Rachel Grundfast it is because I pestered her the most when I was in the office, usually at times when she needed urgently to be doing something else, and because of her unfailing courtesy under these uninvited pressures. Jane Good at Music Sales in London kindly made published scores available, and Sally Nevrkla at Warner Music provided promotional copies of the Nonesuch recordings. Final thanks go to Iain MacGregor, successor to Jeff Hudson at Sanctuary, for encouragement in the final stages of writing and for coping with a wobbly schedule during an unexpectedly demanding time; and to my partner Priti Paintal and daughter Alisha for many uncomplaining hours of staring at a closed workroom door.

Scene 1
How To Listen

Yes, really. How to listen is crucial. The ear must come before the eye. All books on music need a section about this but hardly any have one. You are supposed to know already. If the subject is Mozart or Tchaikovsky, then that is simply taken for granted. If it is a 'difficult' composer famous for the public's resistance, the stance is more subtle. You apparently agree that the music is a good thing, otherwise you would be reading something else, and it is accepted that you may need help. The elucidation then moves on to analysis, which shows how ingeniously the composer uses his or her material but never says why.

What if it is a composer so direct and clear that there can surely be no misunderstanding? We always bring preconceptions with us, and when we first encounter a piece of music by Philip Glass or anybody else we will have them at the ready. We expect different things of music in different circumstances. Suppose you are at the cinema. You probably do not listen to the music in the film from the front of your mind. You may stop looking at the title sequence by the time it gets down as far as the composer, or you forget the name by the time the film is over. The experience of a successful film is a union of what is seen, heard and felt. If the music stands out, it may be because it reinforces the images and the dialogue, or it may be that it is doing its job too well. More people have heard Glass's music on the soundtrack of *The Truman Show* than in any other way. Most of them do not know who wrote it and many will not remember much about it. If they hear it again after a while, it may sound familiar. But they will be hard pressed to remember why.

Probably this audience is the one that misunderstanding has touched the least. The music will have done the specific job it was meant to do. If people disliked the film they will have said it was because of the story or the acting or the direction. If they liked it they probably accepted the music without thinking about it. If the film really engaged them then the music will have sunk in without their knowing.

Now change the setting. You are no longer in a cinema but in a concert hall. The Philip Glass Ensemble is playing excerpts from, say, an album called *Powaqqatsi*. You have not heard anything by this composer before but you are used to going to concerts and you have some experience of a range of classical music. You expect certain things: recognizable themes, a sense that they are being developed and taken through a range of keys, then a return to first thoughts towards the end. If you also know some contemporary classical music you will be prepared for rather more hard-edged, abrupt, complex and even clashing material, which may be difficult to follow but that you sense is being transformed as the music goes on, taking the piece to a destination some way distant from its beginnings. What you hear is different from anything else. It has elements of melody and theme, to be sure. But they are very basic and they are apparently repeated over and over. The harmonies are few and they also keep returning. The music does not evolve. There are changes but they are sudden and complete. At the end the piece seems to be in exactly the same place as it was at the beginning. You may think it is wonderful or you may be disgusted. You will not forget.

These two examples are at opposite poles of musical experience, but they have one piece of content in common. The music is the same. The *Powaqqatsi* score is one of the main sources of *The Truman Show* soundtrack. In one place it strikes its audiences as natural, while in the other it gives them a shock. It probably does not even sound the same, subjectively. But it is. The difference is entirely in the mind of the listener. It is brought about by the context, but it is not 'out there', it is internal. The film audience have accepted the music for what it is and absorbed what it was meant to convey. They are better prepared for their next encounter with music by Glass than the concert audience. The concert audience, on the other hand, have to come to terms with more than the direct experience. They have to deal with what they expected it to be in the first place. Then they have to change their expectations.

Nobody is let off this hook. Especially not professional critics, who are as apt as anybody else at ignoring what the music is trying to be and then criticizing it for not being something else. The only difference is that they are doing it in public. Glass's music has had a bad press from many commentators since the 1960s. First it was bad because it was minimal and not trying to be modernist. By the time minimalism had been accepted as a valid form of expression, Glass had moved on to something else. Then his music was bad because it was diluting the purity of his original vision. He just cannot win.

Listening to Glass requires the same attitude as listening to any other music. Patience, an open mind and a willingness to be surprised all help. After that there are two honest ways. One is just to listen and accept it at face value. It is the way most people listen to most music and it is also the best. If you want understanding it will come in good time. But sometimes the music does not let you do that. It makes you react in a puzzled or irritated way and it makes you start to ask questions. This is a feature of the listener, not the music, and it makes the second way necessary. Essentially you have to free your mind of the obstacles that are causing the reaction. If you are so inclined, you can do it by meditation, but for practical purposes a rational route is needed to deal with the questions you are asking. The start of this is to set aside the listening for a while and find out two things: what you expected it to be, and why the music was written in the first place. What was Glass trying to do when he came up with a new musical language for himself and started again from scratch? Only after that does your traditional textbook nuts-and-bolts, how-it-works approach have any point. And you may not need it anyway.

What did you expect, then? A tune? An opera? A symphonic drama like Beethoven's? A struggle with discordant material and convoluted treatment? A song with chorus and refrain? A rock thrash? A jazz number with bouts of improvization in the middle? Somewhere in this range are the traditional boundaries of Western music and you will expect the music you hear in a Western concert to fall within them. If it is not Western then it may well fall outside these, but that seems quite easy to accept. An Indian solo, an African song or a Balinese gamelan will do various things that Western music does not do and, once you have decided that are going to listen, you tend to go with what it does.

If you listen to music by Glass as if it were a performance of world music, you might find it easier to get on the right lines. Of course it is not world music or anything of the kind. It is completely a product of the United States and its resources are as Western as a symphony orchestra – sometimes they *are* a symphony orchestra. But it is not limited by those traditional boundaries. It has not gone outside them; it is on the inside, pushing them outwards. It stretches them in unexpected directions even when it is a symphony. So you have to start by accepting that it will do things that Western music does not do, or rather never did before.

Why does Glass do it? For the full story you will need to turn to the final chapter, but the essence is that his music has its roots in theatre. Glass had a traditional Western training and found that, while it gave him a command of composing skills, it did not fully meet his expressive needs. He had been working with experimental theatre companies and wanted to find an appropriate kind of music for plays by Beckett and Brecht and Genet: plays that, as he puts it, 'take the subject out of the narrative'. Sometimes there is not even a narrative in the sense of telling a story. The authors no longer invite you to identify with the main characters, their sufferings and triumphs, as romantic theatre had done. In their different ways they ask you to look instead at the whole dramatic or poetic situation. The characters become a means to an end instead of an end in themselves. There is a parallel in music. Throughout the 19th and early 20th centuries, Western music had been about individual, subjective expression: it put the subject, so to speak, into the narrative. Glass was aware that this content in music put it at odds with the expression of the plays. How could he take it out again? How could he make it express something different from the subjective experience?

His answer was to put music together in a different way. If the 'subject' was being expressed through melodies, tonal progressions, crescendos and climaxes, then they had to go. The building blocks would be the smallest basic elements of music: notes, beats, a tempo. The organizing principle for building with them would be rhythm. He got the idea of giving this role to rhythm from the structure of north Indian classical music. That idea was all he took – there was no question of his trying to write in an Indian style, and his music borrows none of the sounds or melodies or actual rhythms. But it was enough: the missing link. Everything on the surface of the music was either his own invention or, at most, 'in the air' – a number of American composers were pursuing different versions of a simple, fresh start. What happened as a piece unfolded was the repetition and gradual expansion of musical patterns made up from his basic building blocks.

To start with, that was almost all he used. The first attempts at composing this way were made for plays performed by American expatriates in Paris. Later, in New York, he formed his own ensemble to specialize in the music's peculiar demands, which for the performers included an even flow of notes, lots of counting and no let-up. The Philip Glass Ensemble began to give concerts and attracted a cult following. It was the late 1960s and the time when the vogue word came onto the scene that was to dog Glass ever after:

minimalism. For a few short years Glass did indeed compose minimalist music and it brought him widespread attention. It is largely for this that his name appears in histories of 20th-century music and, while the music is not often played live now, it is still listened to on recordings and talked about. The sound is unmistakable, an insistent and relentless blend of electronic organ tone and acoustic instruments delivering a steady musical line, or lines, at an unchanging pace. And sometimes at great length. There is no harmony as such, and the lines are just lines, without forming into the ebb and flow of a melody. They repeat, then they extend. They go through cycles of expansion and contraction. They may turn upside-down. If there are several lines, they may go through cycles of different lengths simultaneously and the piece will then run until all the cycles end at the same time.

How to listen? Accept what you are hearing and let it lead you its own way. You can follow the expansion of phrases if you like. You can switch attention from one part to another, you can observe when cycles begin and end or you can absorb the cumulative effect. Do not expect the same subjective emotion that comes from listening to conventionally expressive music. There are no climaxes and no low points. Instead it reveals two unexpected expressive qualities, which emerge after you have been listening for a while. However fast it moves, it develops a massive calm and certainty. And however abrasive and in-your-face the sound, it seems to have a character of quiet inner joyousness. These are unusual areas of experience for Western music to combine and to make central. They occur in passing in some composers' music, the former in Bruckner for instance and the latter in Bach, but they are usually subordinate to more urgent and unsettled qualities. They are what you take away from a sympathetic listening to music by Glass and in this form they are unique to it.

What to listen to? The epic work is *Music In Twelve Parts*, which lasts for several hours and is, in many ways, a summation of what Glass was trying to do up until the early 1970s. The 'twelve parts' refers both to the number of lines and to the number of sections. Originally it was just the lines. Glass tells the story that he composed the first section as a piece in its own right and played it to a friend. Very good, said the friend, now what about the other 11 parts? He took that as a challenge and the rest of the score followed. For prospective listeners, the sheer length can be daunting and it is a good idea for newcomers to consider the album that contains a number of shorter pieces from this time. They include *Music In Fifths* and *Music In Similar Motion*, two classic examples of minimalism in its heyday, which are much sparer in texture than *Music In Twelve Parts* but correspondingly easier to grasp as a whole.

The music of that period is essential Glass and it is as far as some listeners have ever gone. What followed does not seem so different at first, but over the decades it has continued to evolve until it has reached a kind of music that is only distantly related, in the way that a great-grandchild might bear a family resemblance to the first generation. The attitude and the content change. So it follows that the listening practices need to change too. This is another unusual trait for a composer, and it is one that professional listeners have once again found it harder to deal with. Glass is well aware of the situation and has strong views about it:

PG: 'The true minimalism was really over by the end of *Music In Twelve Parts,* completed in 1974. If you look in the history books and the university curricula, they tend to write about those pieces because that's what they know. There's 25 years of music that they're missing. If I wrote music that was important enough to be considered before I was 40, surely the music should be considered that I wrote between 40 and 65. I don't really care what people say, it doesn't matter to me at all. What does matter to me is when things are so badly represented that it becomes stupid. If people act professionally then I think they should take the responsibility to deal with the subject in a completely intelligent way.'

There is a consensus among academics and critics to deal with music from a certain point of view – this became stuck in the history that went through the Second Viennese School and on to Boulez, and it still dominates the European perspective:

PG: 'I was in Austria recently [to give a lecture at the Universitat Mozarteum Salzburg: it was followed by audience questions, mostly about minimalism!] and talking to people there a lot, and I would say there are three kinds of musical writers that I've come across. There are people who are real musicologists, people with PhDs in modern music or renaissance music, and they are equipped to teach courses in history and to write papers; they make their livelihood mostly in universities. Then there's another kind of writers who are actually music critics, and those kinds of writers have the background and experience to write intelligently – whether they do or not is another question but they are literate about music, some of them can play the piano and they can read music and they tend to be hired in the better papers and magazines. That's just a tendency, I wouldn't say that's universally true. The third, which we mostly find, are what I call music journalists. They are basically the guys that cover fires and wars and rapes and burglaries, and we have people in the music business who operate on that level. Some call them music journalists and that's what they do, they're not necessarily qualified, sometimes they can take on the responsibility for making judgments which are way beyond their capacity but they do it anyway. And it turns out that they can't read music, even, they don't have any equipment, they have no entrée to the work.

'That's not necessarily a bad thing. Shaw wrote music criticism, I think he knew his music though some of his opinions were rather coarse. He didn't appreciate Verdi, he didn't understand a lot of the European operatic music of his time very well – he didn't like it; but he did seem to have some education in music. The trouble is that kind of education doesn't guarantee that you know anything very intelligent. Fortunately Shaw is remembered for his other writings, though his music criticism has been printed and you can still buy it. The thing that all these people have in common is that they write about music, so you're liable to find that they're writing anywhere, and the poor unsuspecting reader may have no way of knowing to what degree the writer is qualified.

'There are people writing on major papers in the United States who come from the sports section, or they come from the gardening. It's common in cities in America that are not the major cities, where they have one or two papers, for the entertainment writer to cover sports, theatre and music. Sometimes that's not too bad because you get an honest opinion, but the fact of the matter is that I rarely read reviews because most of my concerts are on the road. I do a concert, I leave the next day and I never see the papers. While I can read in Portuguese and French, I don't read in German and Dutch, so I have no idea what those people are writing. I was just in Scotland doing a couple of concerts and they said, you were reviewed, we'll show the review to you tomorrow, but the next day I forgot to ask about it and they didn't mention it, so I never saw it. I have no idea whether it was a good review or a bad review.

'In fact it makes very little difference to my mind. It doesn't sell tickets to my concerts, the concerts are over by the time I get the review. Record reviews rarely sell records, as you know; record reviews don't have the impact on sales the way theatre reviews can. To a degree I think literary reviewers have some impact on book sales. There's very little impact on the public with music reviewers. Newspapers feel they have to have it, and it's nice for the writers to be able to make a living one way or the other. So my personal feeling is that it makes very little impact on my life as a composer, and I don't pay a lot of attention to it. Even the musicologists very often are writing from a perspective which is 20 or 30 years out of line with what's going on. Often, they're not very much in touch.

'You do have good writers. We have several in America who write generally about cultural affairs. They're very good at talking about the state of American culture and that might include film and music, and the good ones are well educated in the theatre arts and the musical arts and the plastic arts. They can be quite interesting. But these aren't really reviewers. They write books about American culture – where we are as a nation and a people, how we're functioning. People who write about culture have a much better chance of being listened to than people who simply write about music. If you're prepared to talk about modern painting and modern music and modern film at the same time, you do get a better grasp of what's going on.'

So much for the music press... As the following chapters will show, Glass has taken up new musical challenges for several reasons but they do not include other people's opinions – or only in so far as musicians and other artists who like his music have continually pressed him to write for them or work with them. The challenge that was to prove most productive of all, opera, came to him first through a collaboration and then a commission. Since he was a composer with a passion for working in theatre, he was always likely to show up in the opera house eventually. His first opening, however, was one of his fruitful accidents. The collaboration that led to it was with the radical theatre and performance art director Robert Wilson. Very much on the same 'non-narrative' wavelength, the two conceived the one-of-a-kind piece *Einstein On The Beach* for a tour of European summer theatre festivals in 1976 using a company of actors formed for the purpose along with the Philip Glass Ensemble. With musicians integrated into the action and stage design that took the visual content out of its supporting role and put it on equal terms with the performance arts, the formidably long work was a hit with the avant-garde theatre public and was crucial in advancing Wilson's career in Europe. When it was taken to the United States in the autumn, however, it was booked into the Metropolitan Opera House. This theatre was then, as it remains now, a bastion of artistic conservatism. The Met ran its own season from Monday to Saturday and was available for other shows on Sunday, and it was for two Sundays that it hosted *Einstein On The Beach*. The work reached the theatre public it was seeking and became a New York sensation. It made Glass's name overnight in a much more public arena than he had been used to. But because this was the Met, it was also seen by opera followers and the opera establishment. Suddenly *Einstein On The Beach*, much to its composer's surprise, was an opera. And being a New York sensation, it had to be the most revolutionary opera for decades.

The issue of whether the piece was an opera had been arising throughout the European tour. As in New York it had been performed mostly in opera houses because these were the spaces that had the technical resources to deal with its stage demands. Debate flourished about what the work was. Glass said that he tended to agree with people who said it was not an opera at all, and that at the time he thought the operatic tradition was essentially dead. He was more interested in starting from a more vital point such as Wilson's work. The director of the Netherlands Opera, who saw *Einstein On The Beach* in Amsterdam, had a different starting point. He asked Glass whether he would like to write 'a real opera'. Glass, who had never seen himself doing anything of the kind, had to think. What did a real opera mean? It turned out to mean a work to be performed by people whose skill and experience lay in the operatic field. He was not at all interested in the operatic tradition as such. On the other hand he liked the practical and theatrical possibilities offered by the opera houses he had been visiting, with their large size and their human and physical resources. So he accepted the challenge and set to work.

Satyagraha, the work that resulted, proved to be the start of the most successful and the best-documented opera-composing career in the second half of the 20th century. Glass is even credited with rescuing the art form from stagnation, given the lack of impact and diminishing quantity of other contemporary operas. As time has gone by he has become at ease with the thought of being an opera composer as part of his life as a theatre musician. For this chapter, however, the crucial point about his starting to write for opera companies is that it reinforced developments that were already happening in his music as a whole. In the not too distant future, the art of listening to it would have to change dramatically too.

The first move had been made a year before *Einstein On The Beach*. It was a piece called *Another Look At Harmony* and the title is a literal description of what is most important within it. Until then the only harmony was the product of interacting lines of music. Now there were chords. But the chords had a very particular function: they were there to underline the rhythmic movement. Instead of rhythm supporting melody and harmony as in previous Western music, the situation was back to front. The rate of change of the harmony, or harmonic rhythm as musical analysts like to call it, was more important than the harmonic content. So it was 'another look' in two senses. From there, Glass took the idea straight on to the music of *Einstein On The Beach* and gave the score one of its most memorable features: apparently endless repeats of the same five chords, in gradually changing rhythms.

You cannot exactly avoid listening to the chords. They turn up over and over again in *Einstein On The Beach*, with their distinctive progression of harmonies and their top line that becomes like a melodic tag. As they come round you are therefore listening immediately to the rhythm and its changes. There is no 'how to listen' because what you hear is what the music is. It is worth bearing in mind that the rhythm has priority over the harmony if you catch yourself wondering why the chords keep repeating. But otherwise it is just a matter of letting the progressions build up into substantial structures.

The reappearance of harmony also turned out to be important for another reason. It started getting Glass interested in harmony again. He carefully chose the chord sequence because it had an inbuilt ambiguity; it begins in one key and ends in another and it gets there by pivoting on a chord that has two meanings – one in relation to the chords before it and a different one in relation to what follows. It was fascinating in its own right and it proved to be the start of many things to come. Other harmonies became interesting. And once he had been asked to write *Satyagraha* for a conventional opera company he had to face a second departure. What would the singers sing? In *Einstein On The Beach* the singers were members of the ensemble and they sang, essentially, rhythms expressed through syllables. Solo opera singers would expect something else: melody. It might be an awkward and angular melody following the tradition of Alban Berg, the most accomplished opera composer of the Schoenberg followers. Or it might be an extension of the lyrical tradition of Verdi and Puccini. Or it might be something else again. But a melodic line would have to be there.

Looking back in 1990 Glass told an interviewer that he felt 'lucky' that *Satyagraha* had worked out well for the voices. He had not been intending to become an opera composer and yet the music turned out to be suitable. He even said he 'didn't deserve to have written so well' and emphasized that a decade later, with much more experience, he knew more and did it better. The source of his luck, he thought, was that he had sung in a chorus as a student and had developed a feel for that. He has called *Satyagraha* a choral opera, and it features a musical development that works particularly well with that somewhat oratorio-like implication. This development is related to a form that comes straight out of musical history: the chaconne. In the traditional form, a staple of the 17th and 18th centuries, a bass line repeats over and over, while overlaying parts are gradually added and varied, forming a predominant harmonic pattern, which in turn can be varied. The parallel with Glass's introduction of repeating chord sequences is clear. Patterns can be built up over a substantial time scale by extending phrases and introducing additional parts.

The music suggests that by taking 'another look at harmony' Glass did rather more than just starting to use chords. He opened the door only slightly, but opened it all the same, to taking another look at anything else he had left out of his minimalist music. Now it seemed that he was deliberately leaving the door ajar. With hindsight he turns out to have propped it open by using the thin end of a wedge. For two decades it would keep opening a little further, and this is the key to listening to the music he was writing then.

How to listen should really, for the central part of Glass's work, become 'go and see'. This is the most innovative opera composer of recent times and there is no remotely close substitute for a direct experience of the work in the round. A few of his operas are starting to become available on DVD, and there are very rare television broadcasts in most Western countries. This is the next best thing although it has to be tempered by the fact that the necessary technology is not available to everybody, while the interval between broadcast opportunities in any one country may be several years even on specialist digital channels. Going and seeing is in itself not a practical option for the majority of the population, unless they live within reach of an opera house that has a policy of staging contemporary work and have the means to acquire what are usually expensive tickets. Once again the interval between productions may well be several years again, or they may simply be a one-off. Even in London, which has two of the more adventurous established venues in the world, the English National Opera has put on just two of them over a period of 15 years, and the currently supportive Barbican Centre is restricted to smaller-scale works.

It has to be said that the Barbican in 2001–03 is becoming one of the few European venues that is attempting to promote Philip Glass as he is now in something like a full perspective. Within a period of 15 months it will have hosted the European première run of the opera *Galileo Galilei*, the British premières of two symphonies plus the European première of the *Concerto Fantasy* and the extensive touring retrospective series *Philip On Film*. Even before this, it had accommodated one of the few showings of the ill-fated multi-media collaboration with Robert Wilson, *Monsters of Grace*, never fully completed and now unlikely to be presented again. If this commitment to his work continues, then Londoners at least may be able to 'go and see' without requiring a bank loan.

A perspective on the operas as a whole is practically impossible to acquire because they have been commissioned by an international spread of theatres. Almost certainly nobody outside Glass's immediate circle has seen all of them, or even a majority. The content of the present book has been fundamentally determined by this situation. The author is in the same position as readers in that it is impossible for him to attend more than a small number of stage productions of Glass's work. He has to rely on reports of the rest backed up by some experience of the music, videos and photographs. The first three, a trilogy of 'portrait operas' including *Akhnaten* as well as *Einstein On The Beach* and *Satyagraha*, have been much written about and are already historical works. As for the rest, coverage is piecemeal and patchy and largely a matter of press articles. It seems to be impossible for any one writer to make a balanced, honest and reliable survey of this output in full. No attempt has therefore been made to present it in detail. Unless the composer himself were to write such a survey – perhaps as a follow-up to his book *Music By Philip Glass* (also published as *Opera On The Beach*) in which he looked back on the trilogy fairly soon after it was complete – it will have to wait either until somebody can physically get around to productions of everything, if they are all ever staged again, or as second-best case until everything or nearly everything can be seen on screen.

The effect is that Glass's priorities in musical and theatrical forms cannot be matched by anybody else. We experience his work initially from the opposite end of the telescope, led by recordings of instrumental music and increasingly orchestral music, with an occasional foray to the theatre if we are lucky and more often to the cinema. An interesting phenomenon is now under way in which this becomes the shared viewpoint and Glass's position is unique. The shared viewpoint is reinforced by his continuing to be prolific in the non-theatre genres, so that they are more and more substantial in their own right. Which is true, which is false? The distinction becomes meaningless because, for the audience, only one viewpoint is available. This book has had to work from it, and it has even been strengthened by the fact that the author was able to get right up to date – at least from archive recordings of live performances – on the concert works. Glass himself talks about the phenomenon in interview material presented mainly in the chapter about symphonies (see pp.72–6).

What it means for this chapter is that the 'go and see' advice is idealistic. Mostly, you will not be able to. Another option is to get hold of two of his cult movies from the 1980s, *Koyaanisqatsi* and *Powaqqatsi*, directed by Godfrey Reggio. The third part of an intended trilogy, *Naqoyqatsi*, planned over many years, was completed in 2002 and may be showing in art house cinemas by the time this book is published. In these films there is no dialogue, the creative dynamic is between images and music and the collaboration between the artists was close to the extent that the film was partly planned to follow the music, which in turn was based on the images in preliminary footage. This is as close to the condition of opera as another medium is likely to get, and in the cinema it is a different experience from the movies that use Glass's music conventionally as part of their soundtrack. But it is not that close. For a start, it is conceived predominantly for instruments, with voices in a subsidiary or choral role. The film has a different dimension of wholeness in that the images themselves are organized in a kind of visual rhythm. They recur, they evolve gradually, they are speeded up and slowed down. Their style is like a visual parallel to Glass's at the time. The music of *Koyaanisqatsi*, however, has had an enduring life on record beyond the time-span of a soundtrack album, and it is written densely enough to hold the attention. If videos or showings of the films are hard to find, you may well find yourself listening to the score on its own.

How to listen? The CD on its own is slightly compromised in that the music is divided up into sections reflecting the course of the film. But the sections are longer than in *Powaqqatsi* and the music has time to go through characteristic processes. The music for the title sequence features a short repeating section, which intones the name of the film – a Hopi word that suggests life out of balance – over a strong bass line: the chaconne idea, stripped down. Later, fast passages put broken chord figures through harmonic progressions that mark out the rhythmic structure, like a wider-ranging version of processes in *Einstein On The Beach*. Elsewhere Glass provides freer passages in an unusual (for him) diversity of instrumental colours. He has talked about conceiving 'analogous or allegorical musical images': to go with clouds, for instance, 'large, slow-moving clusters of brass'. Glass makes the point that clouds are not supposed to somehow 'sound' like brass; what is important is that using brass becomes 'a convincing artistic decision'. Correspondingly, if you listen to the music on its own you are not required to imagine clouds as you listen, they are just the reason the musical material is as it is and the track title 'Cloudscape' is there to point you in that direction if you happen to be curious. The music works well enough for listeners who are not aware of the title and that is a measure of how convincing the artistic decision was.

Whether you 'stay in and listen' to some of Glass's operatic music, or whether you can 'go and see', if you know anything of what he had been writing before you will be unable to miss some of the changes that were happening to his music. The wedge in the door that he had opened was pushed in a little further by the nature of an opera company. He had to write something for his singers. Unless he wanted them to go back to first principles and sing like the singers in *Einstein On The Beach*, that meant a vocal line. The door had admitted melody.

What is striking is that the melodic lines are immediately very straightforward, quite simple and lyrical – almost conventional, even old-fashioned. Glass could have gone in several directions. He could have chosen spectacular virtuosity and vocal display. He could have latched onto avant-garde techniques and fragmented lines, as in the vocal music of many of his European contemporaries. He could have persisted and extended the *Einstein On The Beach* style in ways unknown, or could have come up with something different again. But he chose what might have been the least expected solution. He has often said that by his mid-20s he had absorbed what composers had done in extending vocal techniques and found he had no wish to work with those techniques. He always found them interesting, he said, but just not for him – they made him think he would be putting musical invention at the service of technique, rather than the other way round.

The arrival of vocal melody means that Glass's operatic scores are inevitably listened to first through the voice, which is underpinned by his personal musical processes. Maybe they were worked out the other way around, with the voice floated above the process, but what you experience most immediately is the human being addressing you. Over several years, other features appeared in the operatic scores: more orchestral colour, more variety of pace and a much more extensive harmonic range. The music from *Akhnaten* onwards starts to have prevailing key areas, and contrasting episodes outside them. Eventually the vocal lines became more complex and demonstrative when required, still without actively pandering to the egos of opera singers instead of their musicality.

Music continued to be placed at the service of the dramatic situation. It was when Glass's orchestral scores started to come into their own that the enrichment of the musical language became a foreground feature in a big way. The music had to tell its own story. Compared with his instrumental music of the 1970s, it had a whole repertoire of resources to use that he did not even want before. It sounds familiar on two levels. On the one hand, it is unmistakably the work of its composer. The basic building blocks remain elemental: lightly syncopated chords, arpeggios and broken chords, scale patterns. On the other hand, the music takes in new elements that belong to the older Western tradition – orchestral and instrumental colour, variety of texture, dynamic light and shade, melody – and recently new expressive areas from the intensely agitated to the positively luxuriant. But on both levels the effect of the music is quite different from what has gone before. It does more than you expect of his earlier music and less than you expect of a classical symphony. The 'more' may be obvious but the 'less' continues to be a product of his music's aesthetic aims and methods of organization. Glass has admitted many traditional features but is still happy to do without Beethoven-style tonal tension, long-approached climaxes or rhetorical emphasis. For all its greater diversity of means, it continues to embody the even and steady flow that has enthralled or irritated its listeners ever since Glass started composing professionally.

The irritation factor is undeniable and appears to be caused by the lack of tonal tension and rhetoric. This applies to the minimalist pieces and to the recent concert works alike. It appears, on the basis of many years' experience, to be at the root of critical rejection. If the yardstick of your musical judgment is the Western tonal tradition of the 18th and 19th centuries, then the minimalist music is unacceptable because it rejects the tradition, and the latest music is rather tame because it brings back some parts of the tradition in an apparently cautious way, but is insufficient to generate the binding force of classical-style tonal tension. A kind of double-think prevails, causing opinions to be uttered that would not be held about music the critic likes.

Here for instance is the review in *Gramophone* magazine of the recording of *Symphony No 5*: 'the music simply isn't varied enough to reflect the enormous differences in meaning, spirit and stylistic complexion that are so powerfully spelt out in the texts' (the texts are a compilation made from worldwide spiritual traditions – see pp.93–6). This opinion reflects a prejudice that the music ought to have set out to be more varied, or that it has tried and failed. What about that favourite critics' concept, stylistic integrity? Do not critics praise composers they like for the way that the music's stylistic integrity unifies a diverse variety of sources? Do they not complain that music with too much variety of its own 'lacks stylistic integrity'? Prejudice makes the opinion dependent on the person about whom it is held. And this *Gramophone* review is by a critic who had written sympathetically about previous symphonies and evidently enjoyed them. In fairness, it should be added that he then suggests Glass may have intended to make the music subordinate to the text. But the damage was already done.

How to listen to the recent music, in the present author's opinion, involves continuing to suspend your expectations about traditional Western classical music. Just because Glass's music sounds more traditional, from moment to moment, it does not have to behave traditionally. You can even enjoy it, now, for some of the reasons that you enjoy Tchaikovsky: melody, emotion, sensuous colour. But the music adds up in a different way. It does not argue; it exists. For this author, Glass's music at all stages has been about states of being rather than about conflict. It seems paradoxical to say that a consummate composer for the theatre writes fundamentally non-dramatic music, but it is that very quality that makes it so effective. The music offsets, complements and goes beyond the drama. It becomes dramatic by association, rather than from its inherent qualities. Glass has also preferred theatrical forms that differ from traditional drama. The musical style began in the company of non-narrative theatre. It continued with musical theatre that 'takes the subject out of the narrative' and with opera scenarios that are more concerned with exploring the meaning, iconic status and cultural significance of individuals, such as Gandhi or Einstein, than with the surface drama. Even the relatively dramatic content of *Galileo Galilei* is given a characteristic twist by featuring significant events of his life in reverse order. The central character is therefore revealed rather than developed.

With concert works it is the same: the material is again revealed rather than developed. Different kinds of material are set in contrast rather than engaged in argument. Whereas the symphony in classical music is the most dramatic of orchestral forms, expressing itself through tonal conflict, symphonies by Glass are put together partly from material that extends and proliferates like his earlier music, and partly from an intricate pattern of sections of music that alternate and replace one another. Concertos have a dramatic content simply from the spectacle of soloists being placed in front of an orchestra – but the material works in the same way as the symphonies do.

What to listen to? Start with *The Light*, his first work for orchestra alone. It was premièred by the Cleveland Orchestra conducted by Christoph von Dohnanyi in 1987, and the commission was for a specific occasion: the centenary of 'the Michelson-Morley experiment', a pioneering study of the speed of light that preceded and made possible the theories of Einstein. Glass conceived the music as a tone poem, a complement to his 'portrait operas'. He has called it 'a portrait not only of the two men for whom the experiments are named but also that historical moment heralding the beginning of the modern scientific period.' As this description suggests, it is different from the kind of tone poem that tells a story, like those by Liszt and Strauss. It is part reflection and part high-speed fantasy. The music begins with slow, spaced groups of chords enclosing a melody that features an eight-note repeated phrase, and moves on to typical broken-chord figure. After five minutes it moves up-tempo. The material consists of several patterns with distinctive rhythms, which are often separately allocated to woodwind, brass or strings. The patterns alternate and displace one another over bass lines that remain constant except when big chords sweep across the whole orchestra. Some patterns recur unchanged, some evolve. The result is an impression of stasis at great speed. There are dynamic peaks in the middle and towards the end: after the second, the music suddenly introduces a pulsing note at a low pitch and the patterns gradually dissolve over it. The themes of the slow introduction appear at the fast tempo, mixed in with the fast section's own material, and the music fades down to silence.

The Light is a prototype for many of Glass's orchestral works only it uses a simpler range of materials, which make it quite easy to hear how they are treated. Shifting relationships between musical patterns are at the heart. The music examines the 'state of being' of these patterns by offsetting them against others. Any sense of debate or dialectic, such as you find in the working-out of symphonies from Haydn through to Mahler and beyond, is absent. If you have the experience of this piece in your mind when you listen to Glass's subsequent orchestral works, you will be well placed to listen to them for what they are, without false expectations.

All generalizations are made to be broken, and the one about drama is no exception. A more inherently dramatic quality has appeared in his solo voice parts. One of the best examples is even in a symphony, his latest, only now starting to get performances. It is too soon to say whether this is an exception or a sign that another new phase of Glass's music has begun. There is, for the moment, a drawing together of Glass's theatre works and his concert works that may be a pointer to the future. But nobody knows for sure – not even the composer until he writes the future for himself because, as the following chapters will continue to show, the music has a habit of going its own way and surprising everybody.

Scene 2
Galileo And Other Collaborators

Surveying Glass's work is something of a crash course in the history of science. Einstein, Stephen Hawking (see below), the relatively obscure Albert Michelson and Edward Morley (see p46), and now Galileo, all figure. The opera *Galileo Galilei* was premièred on 24 June 2002 in Chicago. As with his other works it is a long way from straight narrative biography set to music, and it uses key episodes from the subject's life in a singular way. If you need a bluffer's guide to Galileo it goes like this: in the early 17th century he was one of the first observers of the night sky to use a telescope, which showed him the movements of Jupiter's moons, and he worked out a scientific argument that the planets, including Earth, orbited the Sun. Received wisdom and Christian teaching held that God created Earth to be the centre of the universe and that all the contents of the sky revolved around it. The doctrine had been questioned before, notably by Copernicus, but only on a theoretical basis.

Now there was physical evidence. It involved a mathematical understanding of gravity, a subject on which Galileo had conducted many experiments including a famous one that involved rolling balls down inclined planes. His arguments brought him into political conflict with the Catholic Church, which was engaged through the Inquisition in suppressing opponents. After a show trial, Galileo was forced to confess to heresy, recant his proofs and affirm that Earth stood still at the centre. Immediately after uttering this coerced lie he said, under his breath, 'And yet, it moves' – a dramatic way of clearing his conscience before God in the face of the deity's representative on Earth.

RM: 'Why did you choose Galileo?'

PG: 'I came across a series of essays by Alfred North Whitehead, and one chapter was on Galileo. He wrote that Galileo was blind when he died. I had studied Galileo when I was a student, I had read some of the works and we were even made to re-do his experiments, those inclined-plane ones. When I read that, I just thought it was an extraordinary fact [Galileo's blindness was probably caused by glaucoma and cataracts – not looking at sunspots through the telescope, as was once believed] which I had somehow overlooked, and I would say that I got the idea for the opera almost immediately from that one statement.

'My first thought was, what was he thinking? What kind of thoughts was he having for that one year, it was, that he was blind? I immediately translated it to the stage and I saw the first scene of the opera as being the old man, with his telescope, who was blind, and it would be a long soliloquy of some kind about how that had happened. He was a very religious man as you know. His argument with the Church was that he thought the human mind was a gift of God so that we could understand the world, and that his work was, through his researches, his science, to demonstrate the beauties of the world, which was God's work. Yet there he was, it could be he wondered why he ended up blind. Did he see something he wasn't supposed to see?

'It raises the whole issues of the trial and his conversations over again. He might have had some doubts. I wrote another opera earlier called *The Voyage*, which was about Columbus, and in the second act of the opera Columbus has almost the same monologue or soliloquy, where he becomes very discouraged. He's in the middle of the ocean, he thinks they're lost and he goes into a kind of reverie. I saw the Galileo opera working this way: what will happen is that he began to remember his life, and he began to see his life in reverse. As he remembered the scene, the lights came on at the centre of the stage and he could see the scene. He was seeing in his memory, so his vision would be confident. I wrote eight or nine scenes and in my first version it ends up with him as a young man constructing his telescope. Then at the end of the opera you have the young man with the telescope and the old man with the telescope, so you needed two Galileos. At the beginning he's a tenor and later he becomes a baritone; the baritone fits better with the dynamic quality of his youth, as an old man his voice is a little more feeble.

'I met with the writer and director Mary Zimmerman – she wanted to do the piece, I'd told her about it – and she suggested that we have a further scene with him as a little boy singing in an opera of his father's, and I agreed to that. There was the trial, of course – the recantation and then the trial – and one scene we called 'The Lamp', which was a well known event where he was in the church with his daughter and he was looking at the pendulum, the lamp swinging, and he was timing it by counting the pulse, using that as a measure [the pendulum effect is a consequence of the force of gravity]. There is another scene with Barberini, the guy that became Pope Urban VIII, a cardinal then. It ends up being ten scenes, about 90–95 minutes long. Mary and Arnold Weinstein [author, experienced lyricist and teacher of American literature] wrote the libretto, based on the sketch I gave them. I supplied the sketch outlining the idea of the opera, they wrote elaborated on that and then I worked on it some more to get the text suitable for singing.'

RM: 'One of the interesting things about Einstein and also about Columbus was that they are people who have a heroic image, and yet there's something that is deeply flawed going on through there as well. Did you find anything like that in Galileo? I can see there's a parallel with his reaction to blindness...'

PG: 'There's another one too. I did some music for a film about Stephen Hawking called *A Brief History Of Time*, and I got interested in scientists as these singular brave people: the ones that were working on the edge of science like Einstein and like Galileo, they were bound to have those moments of doubt, but they must have had a lot of confidence to have done it to begin with. People like that are interesting because they are extremely brave people but they must have had trouble with someone. The human elements come up a lot in this piece. You don't see it very much in *Einstein*, that's a rather more abstract piece. There's always been interest in Galileo, there's a fairly famous play by Brecht, he was a charismatic character.

'The thing about operas is they're not history, they're art, so we're allowed to tamper with it to a certain degree, but it's very speculative, isn't it? It's not meant to be a documentary. There is a story here, it's the story of his life, but it's done in reverse, so it goes from darkness to light. The music goes, not exactly the same way, but the end of the opera is a make-believe scene from one of his father's operas, which of course it really wasn't, and Mary used the story of Orion and Eos. [Orion the handsome hunter and adventurer, blinded in revenge for a past crime, wins the love of Eos who persuades her brother Helios to restore his sight; he is inadvertently killed by Artemis, who atones by placing him among the stars.] She gives this mythic side to it. The end of the opera is quite beautiful in a way, because you see the old man and the young boy and the young Galileo, the three of them are there and it's totally about Galileo. What she is saying is that Galileo ended up being in the stars, he became immortal in a certain way. So it's rather romantic at the end, very uplifting; you see Galileo becoming part of the heavens.

'But at the beginning he's just this old man who is blind, who can't leave his house and hasn't been able to explain himself very well to the Church – which had other issues going on. We have to remember there was the Reformation going on in the north of Europe, they really couldn't tolerate that kind of dissent happening at home. He seems to have been a close friend of the guy who became Pope, but in the end the Pope had to choose for politics rather than for even what he might have believed. As we go backward in time we meet the Pope several times, once at the end of the recantation and then again we come across him when he's publishing one of his books and the Pope promises to help him.'

RM: 'Science and religion: you should do Darwin.'

PG: 'I think I'm done with the scientists! I toyed with the idea of Newton but Galileo took care of that for me. The thing about Newton that was interesting is that he was also an alchemist. It would be interesting to do something about Newton that had to do with alchemy, but I've worked with Einstein, with Stephen Hawking and with Galileo and I think that's it.

'As for the music, I knew it had to go from dark to light. Over the years working in the theatre, I did my first play when I was 20 so I've been doing theatre work for 45 years, I've developed some very good tools for working with these kinds of things whether they're narrative or non-narrative. It's not that big a deal, but matching image with music is a big deal. Once the emotive quality of the scene is decided I have the means to make it work the way I want to. It's quite deliberate. Part of it is harmonic and part of it is the way the voices and the music go together, the way the orchestra and the singing go together.'

As this book was being finished, *Galileo Galilei* had just been staged for the first time. It contains more storyline than its predecessors, albeit arranged in its own way, but it evidently belongs to the line of Glass's stage works that are dramatized meditations on the human significance of a great historical figure. Reports suggest that the backward progress through Galileo's life is paralleled not so much in a literal shift from darkness to light as in a steady lightening of mood and a gradual change from slow and quiet to fast and exuberant. Mary Zimmerman's production moves from the realistic to pantomime – for the experiment with balls on an inclined plane – to freewheeling fantasy at the end, when the 'opera within an opera' has Orion taking his place in the stars while the onlookers revolve like planets, and an outbreak of joy in dance and music accompanies Galileo's own appearance in the skies. Joy, perhaps, because the vision embodied in Galileo's discoveries causes his life to shine out above the murky politics that blighted his later years. If so, then the opera's time reversal will have proved an ingenious way to celebrate a triumph of the human spirit over infirmity and malevolence.

Scene 3
Reinventing Symphonies

In the same year that *Einstein On The Beach* hit the world, a different musical scandal was occurring in Britain. The offshore European island, which had not been included in the Einstein première tour around the mainland, learned about the opera's impact rather late when reports started to filter back from the New York performances towards the end of the year. By this time London had had to come to terms with what was happening to one of Britain's very own *enfants terribles*, Peter Maxwell Davies. This was a composer who had made a firebrand's reputation for himself over the previous decade. His method was to use arcane musical processes on medieval or modern material, with results that varied from the impenetrable to the wild, not to say over-the-top: they included an ensemble theatre piece in which a soprano screeched through a loud-hailer, and another that had the protagonist sat on a lavatory while he smeared himself with faeces. Now this other paragon of the mould-breaking avant-garde had come up with something not just shocking, but completely unthinkable. Glass had written a symphony.

The news would not cause a stir today, but that is to take a contemporary perspective. It is difficult to overstate the effect that it had then. Symphonies were something that a progressive artist just did not do. Symphonies were the big traditional classical form that, from the time of Beethoven, defined the summit of musical thinking and achievement for a century and a half. They were written by big traditional classical composers. The biggest of them in recent times, until he died the previous year, was Dmitri Shostakovich. His was not a name you bandied about in smart creative circles, for all his popularity, although there was an element of sympathy in that he was seen as having been kept in a time-warp by the conservative musical requirements of Soviet Russia. Other symphonists included the English oddballs as they were then regarded, Malcolm Arnold and Robert Simpson, and a handful out on the Nordic fringes such as Arvo Part, Eduard Tubin and Aulis Sallinen. There were not many. Even the mainstream Americans had stopped. The species was effectively extinct and nobody who wanted to be taken seriously by the leaders of opinion would touch it.

Had you wished to take a bet that Philip Glass would within 16 years write a symphony, you would have found very good odds. His music stood at the opposite extreme. He had composed symphonic music as a student, but he had abandoned the style for ten years. Since then he had found that his own style was not only durable but capable of extending to lengths beyond the scope of the symphonic tradition. He had just proved that it could also sustain an evening-long collaboration with a creative theatre director that had all the cohesion of opera while rewriting the rules for combining music and stage action. There was surely an agenda and the resources here for a full working life without needing to concern himself with the old ways ever again.

Yet what happened in London with Maxwell Davies proved to be a sign of the times. Not so much the work itself, which despite its composer's talk about the influence of Sibelius proved to be one of his most impenetrable, but the decision to do it. He wrote a series of successors over the following years. Independently, the older Nordic composers started to come in from the cold: in particular Part and Tubin, barely known outside Estonia in the 1970s, became the source of internationally successful recordings. Then the rehabilitation of Arnold and Simpson turned them within their lifetimes – an uncommonly quick change of fortune for Britain – from outsiders shunned by the avant-garde establishment to respected elder statesmen of English music. Within a decade the symphony was no longer a dirty word for a living composer to consider using. Only a few actively did so, but the shift of attitude pointed to a wider underlying change. The avant-garde was beginning to lose its grip and, although some senior composers benefited, and some conservative composers got onto the bandwagon, the dynamic was not a counter-revolution by the old guard. Younger musicians were discovering the joys of music's fundamentals all over again.

Glass never intended to become a symphonist. It was all down to circumstances. The same goes for his other orchestral music, including the growing list of concertos. He has simply responded to commissions. Even now he downplays their importance, because his main concern is with his operas and theatre work. There they are, though: six symphonies in ten years by early 2002, and every sign of more to come. He has now built up a substantial body of symphonic music whose existence tells its own story. It might have been a story of potboilers. Composers have to make their living, and some do it by spending a proportion of their time writing, in a more or less patronizing way, pieces that will pay the rent but do not meet their usual artistic standards. That is not Glass's way. He takes commissions to pay the rent too, but whatever he might think at the prospect of a particular piece, once he starts writing the music takes over. He cannot work frivolously or cynically. The music may be some of his best or it may not, but this has nothing to do with the motivation. So it is that he has come to accept that the symphonic work has a life of its own, almost in spite of himself.

Any observer of the period's music has to notice that Glass's own music was itself partly responsible for changing the climate. The prologue of this book showed the change in microcosm through one person's experience, but the phenomenon was worldwide and in composing it ran well ahead of public perception. It was a reaction against the way in which, at a professional level, a whole world-view was gradually becoming institutionalized. The world-view was that of post-war modernism. Always a minority view, it had come to dominate positions of influence from universities to broadcasting stations to subsidy systems. It did so thanks to the remarkable success of a teacher in France and a summer school in Germany.

The story is so unlikely that it is worth telling here. Just before the Second World War, out of the musical ferment of avant-garde Paris, one name was starting to be spoken of in tones of awe: Olivier

Messiaen. He had belonged to a group of loosely associated composers known as 'La Jeune France', and was beginning to emerge as a true original among originals. The awe was based on respect and bewilderment. He possessed a brilliant mind and a fastidious ear that led him to conceive music of previously unimagined complexity. At the same time he adhered to a fundamentalist Roman Catholicism, which he wanted all of his music to proclaim. The result was that his compositions came out with simple, faith-driven explanations, which half of Europe had had instilled into them by priests since childhood. To the ear they were anything but simplistic, but they had a personal quirk: every so often the dense textures might clarify and something really easy to grasp would occur – a long, sumptuous, sensual tune, or a build-up of massively straightforward harmonies.

You can imagine the split reactions. Fellow composers and musicians would marvel at his technical accomplishments, and sincerely praise him for them, but then they would snigger behind his back at the aura of baby-Jesus naivety that surrounded it. Critics went for the avant-garde intentions but looked down their noses at the frankly tonal climaxes and their Gershwin-like directness. The result was that Messiaen acquired a professional following based on the brilliance of the man and the ingenuity of the music. Meanwhile the public, slow to warm to his music at first, gradually realised that if they were able to sit through the difficult bits, something spectacularly luscious would be along soon. As for the Catholicism, people either took it or left it according to their own beliefs. This meant that Messiaen's music was received in a split-minded way almost exactly opposite to the transcendental unity he intended.

If that were all, the phenomenon would have been interesting but more like a footnote to musical history. When it came to other people's composing, however, his influence on the profession was to be enormous. Some call it disastrous, but that is only with hindsight. The reason is that by all accounts he was a highly accomplished, imaginative and sympathetic teacher, and for many years taught harmony, analysis and composition at the Paris Conservatoire. His classes became a pan-European focus of pilgrimage for creative spirits who wanted to rebel. Nobody planned it. Wise teachers in any case refuse to impose; they have long enough memories to know that the rebellion will occur anyway. They will aim to set standards, but faced with a class of single-minded creative volcanoes, the standards have to be what the students would variously set for themselves if they had the patience or the experience. When enough of these individuals share common ground, some kind of movement is likely to spring up for as long as it suits them.

In a class that contained Pierre Boulez and Karlheinz Stockhausen, the common ground was a radically thought-out attitude rather than a style. All the same the attitude was characteristic. The technical means used by the pre-war serialist composers, chiefly Schoenberg and Webern, became the subject of enthusiastic discussion and analysis. They stemmed from the method that Schoenberg invented in the 1920s for organizing music that was no longer tonal – the '12-note music' still feared by listeners and musicians everywhere. At the time it was influential mainly on his own students, of whom Webern and Berg were the leading ones. The young and ambitious musicians in Paris knew they could take it much further. They could, in fact, systematize everything, and they could continue to do so at inexhaustible length without ever repeating themselves. Webern was a particular icon because of his rigour, though he himself had chosen not to go down this route, which did not fit in with his laconic style. It was left to become a challenge to the brilliant and imaginative. It exerted a further attraction in the context of a Europe recently damaged by ideologies and wars. Physically and socially many of the old ways of living were discredited and there was a hunger for renewal, a necessity for rebuilding and an awareness of technology that could be put to peaceful uses. So too in parts of the creative musical world there was an urge to make a fresh start; to put the old ways to rest and deliberately start again, using some 'technology' that had been devised by far-sighted members of the previous generation, who were no longer around to impose their own ways on rebellious youth.

What did Messiaen pupils do when they graduated? They carried on meeting. The centre was an international summer school in Darmstadt, which was founded in 1946 and continues – with much-diminished impact – to this day. It was the first instance in classical music of a part of the profession starting to organize itself like career scientists. The big cheeses such as Messiaen, the Schoenberg pupil Rene Leibowitz and the Italian avant-garde leader Bruno Maderna would be there. At this annual 'conference' the 'delegates' played and listened to one another's music, read and discussed research papers, and argued vigorously in seminars. During the rest of the year they went back to work in their various 'laboratories', which were in some instances performing groups, in others university jobs and in a few cases, such as Stockhausen's, literally laboratories.

As the school grew, its members began to occupy positions of influence in the musical infrastructure of post-war Europe. This was just the public surface. What really spread the Darmstadt word was the number of minor players on the scene. The experience of attending Darmstadt formed the mind-set of hundreds of intelligent, ambitious musicians who were not destined for prominence as composers or solo performers. These are people who formed ensembles that played new music, wrote about it or obtained jobs in education, public administration, broadcasting and music publishing. Before the idea of networking became fashionable, they were the network. They have been the source of many conspiracy theories about a new music mafia, but the reality is much simpler: they just did their job, according to their conscience, and kept in touch. It is similar to the process that, in a strong political or commercial culture, puts placemen in key positions throughout public life, but with one big difference: people were not cynically 'placed', they were just part of a generation that was on the rise.

Where did these jobs spring from? The public paid for them, often without knowing. In Europe, the world of government funding, expanded higher education, arts bureaucracy and state broadcasting provides a second key to understanding the scene. Idealistically created and motivated, at least in the first instance, it was set up in an attempt to give the citizens access to social and cultural benefits that had been the preserve of the few. Much of it was built after the Second World War, as part of a massive investment in reconstruction. Artistic culture was one area in need of democratizing, and institutions came into being throughout the continent that pursued two aims:

supporting the arts themselves (especially the labour-intensive performing arts) and taking them to a public that had lacked opportunities for artistic experience. They had a need for expert employees who understood the art forms as well as the democratic purpose. Similarly new positions opened up in music sections of broadcasting stations and expanded departments of universities. In a short space of time, a range of opportunities arose for musically literate people who were emerging from their student years not as front-line performers or creators, but possessing a range of specialist knowledge and enthusiasm that suited the tasks of working with music at one remove. Until then, writing, publishing and a limited amount of university teaching had been the main outlets for this kind of second-tier musicianship; few opportunities arose and they were open only to those with the right mix of extra-musical skills. Now there were many more openings. Members of the first generation of trained, committed advocates for the front-line classical music of the mid-century could find a different kind of job – one that had the power to make the music happen.

The dream was to liberate a range of performers and creators from the vagaries of the market and the whims of a patron, and to let them make music for the greater good of everybody. It was, and remains, a dream of astonishing ambition and optimism. Orchestras, opera companies and individual musicians would be secure in their employment, and all sections of society would have access to live musical experience of the highest quality, while the talented would be enabled to pursue a full musical education even when they did not have the means to support themselves fully through long years of training. At the same time, the creative growth of the art would be assured, because the composition of new works would be included under this benevolent umbrella, and composers as well as performers would be taking their place on the state-supported learning curve.

Unfortunately, the dream became corrupted. With hindsight the corruption was inevitable, because there was never enough money for everybody who wanted it. The system required selection and the exercise of power. These were the factors that brought about the rise and fall of the '20th-century music' that became so familiar during the century's final decades, because in narrowing the field down to one that was financially supportable, it also narrowed down the musical options. Judging the claims, making the choices, redirecting the money: traditionally these would be grounds for exercising a Solomon-like wisdom, purified by detachment from the circumstances. The trouble was that it was becoming hard for non-specialist officials or members of committees to grasp the musical issues, particularly when it came to new music as it burgeoned off into the intricate and unfathomable realm of post-war modernism. They needed guidance. They went to the people who knew this world best, the people it had trained. Experts in new music were invited into the system. And that was how the system came to be run by those who benefited from it.

Also with hindsight, the situation was made possible by the very ideals on which it was founded. The 'social and cultural benefits that had been the preserve of the few' remained just that: what the few regarded as social and cultural benefits. The patrician model of handing down culture was not quite outdated at the outset, but it failed to evolve along with the society it served. No thought was given to the possibility that democratizing artistic culture would change the culture itself. But that is always the case with democracy. Once people gain access to the cultural world and its institutions, they will not be content with meekly accepting what they are given; they will seek to use it to propagate their own version of culture. If that world does not broaden of its own accord, people will find their own ways of making it broaden. Those who happen to be running that world at the time have to choose between the world as they know it, and the unruly dangers of opening it up. In music, as with the rest of the arts, the public institutions had been placed in the hands of well meaning liberals who, when faced with the choice, tended to retrench into old patrician ways. Art was what they said it was. The rest was mass culture and not fit for funding.

The full history of these times has yet to be written, although both winners and losers from the period have published plenty of anecdotal vitriol. The consequences in music, however, were soon clear. There was a hierarchy of musical styles, classical at the top, and within the top level there were preferred styles of composing. If you did not use them you would find it harder to be performed, broadcast and published. It was a subtle form of censorship, much less blatant than the requirements of Soviet Russia for socialist realism, but less honest in that nobody took responsibility for it. No single person exercised enough control for that to be possible. It was just the way things were. That was how the musical public had to see it too. The interests of listeners, and even of performers, were decided for them. The fact that new music steadily lost its audience did not matter. The view was that taking account of other people's opinions amounted to selling out – and that was a compromise of artistic integrity.

If nobody was in control, then no single person could change things either. There had to be some kind of united movement and, in the event, there was none. Instead, the system was bypassed. It was a gradual process of disaffection by individuals. They could make no headway, they would not compromise, they just wanted to do things differently; whatever the reason, they found some other outlet. For John Taverner it was the Russian Orthodox Church and the possibility of writing vastly expanded forms of ritual music. For Michael Nyman it was cult film scores, which made tours of the music necessary when it caught on. For Gavin Bryars it was the English experimental tendency and an eccentric choice of subjects, such as speculating on the acoustics of the ship's orchestra on the *Titanic*, which kept playing while the ship sank. For Arvo Part, torn between his symphonic leanings and his avant-garde training, it was a new start using very simple, medieval-style material. For Henryk Gorecki it was the discovery of a highly emotional, slow-moving and cumulative language that tapped into the secret longings of put-upon Poles. In New York, for the rising generation labelled as minimalists, it was the discovery of other cultures' musical priorities and the will to build large spans of music from absolute fundamentals.

For the next generation, the one after Philip Glass's, the options became more diverse. A minority of creative musicians followed the traditional conservatoire training and sought their fortunes in the old world of contemporary music. More people put their energies into high-quality rock music, jazz, free improvization, electronic and computer music and the burgeoning field of dance music that had grown from repetitive and sampling techniques and transformed the old disco repertoire into an astonishing range of club styles. As the populations of the world's cities became more racially and culturally diverse, so the experience of 'world music' changed from something exotic to a home-grown phenomenon, with new dimensions from rap to Parisian rai to British Asian fusion springing up everywhere. They found their audiences, and within less than a generation the world of the self-styled avant-garde had been left struggling to keep up.

All that is another story. For Glass-watchers, the point is that during the time that his career was developing there were the makings of several audiences and performing networks for contemporary music. They include the one that his music helped to shape, a collection of refugees from new classical music more than followers of it, along with some of the public for progressive popular music, enthusiasts for parallel developments in the visual and dramatic arts, and those who were just plain curious. It was an informal and uncontrolled phenomenon, which straddled conventional boundaries and was barely recognized by practitioners in the older forms. It was picked up on first by marketing specialists: in London it became recognizable as 'the Serious mailing list' in allusion to the now long-established production and promotion company Serious, a specialist in boundary-crossing music with a reputation for drawing big audiences.

It was a quite different audience from the traditional one for classical music, which was mostly resistant to new work apart from a minority who specifically followed contemporary classical composers.

This more established audience had no direct exposure to Glass's music, because he had not composed anything for it and the promoters in that area were showing no sign of asking him. All this was to change by the 1990s. The main bridge turned out to be opera: after the success of the anything-but-conventional *Einstein On The Beach*, the 'normal' opera world started to find Glass interesting. How that came about is the story of the sixth chapter. Another bridge was film, in that it brought Glass to work with the Kronos Quartet and led to the extension of his series of string quartets for concert performance. This line was to be limited in its effect, not because the chamber-music public is quite small: Kronos built up their reputation by breaking away from the contemporary classical establishment and playing new music that spoke to much the same audiences that Glass was already starting to reach with ensemble music. Twenty years on, as Kronos themselves became, in effect, the new contemporary establishment, they found that they were playing Glass to a more conventional chamber audience. But by then, Glass's music had found another way into the concert halls.

This was by way of a knock-on effect that the opera connection possessed. Instrumentalists and conductors who work in opera tend to have an active life in the orchestral world and, if they take the initiative in their work rather than waiting to see what they are asked to play, they will create overlaps. A conductor who admires a composer that he or she came across in the opera house will naturally be on the lookout for concert pieces. If there are none, and there is the opportunity to influence the source of a commission for a new work, then the conductor can try to see if the composer could write it. So it was that the name of Dennis Russell Davies came to loom large in Glass's work.

Davies is an American conductor and pianist who has long had an unusually adventurous reputation for the breadth of his repertoire and, in particular, for his energetic commitment to contemporary music, by leading European as well as American composers. Living in Germany since 1980, he has been an active presence on the international opera scene throughout that time. His links with Glass go back to 1978 and the opera that first infiltrated the conventional opera world, *Satyagraha*. He had become music director of the Stuttgart Opera and was on the lookout for contemporary American work. Glass had been commissioned by the Netherlands Opera and was keeping an ear open for further production possibilities. When the two musicians were introduced by a mutual friend, the upshot was that Davies decided to take responsibility for *Satyagraha*'s German première in 1980. Ever since there has been an ongoing musical relationship, with Davies conducting many presentations of Glass operas around the world. Several of them have used a large orchestra, and Glass acknowledges that his experience in orchestral writing stemmed from the rush of commissions that followed their success.

Theatre work remained Glass's central creative preoccupation, and it was Davies who took the lead in pushing him along a path that he had not intended to travel. One of Davies's main US bases was the American Composers Orchestra (ACO), which he had helped to found in 1977, and this proved to be one of the key organizations in giving Glass's orchestral experience a platform of its own. It took several years to come about, while Glass took up the theatre and film invitations that came his way. The ACO was finally able to set up a commission for 1987, which turned out to be the *Violin Concerto*.

Later the same year it was followed by Glass's first mature piece for orchestra alone, *The Light*, which was one of those commissions that came out of the blue from elsewhere – in this case the Cleveland Orchestra and its music director, Christoph von Dohnanyi. Two further works, *The Canyon* in 1988 for the Rotterdam Philharmonic and *Itaipu* in 1989, with chorus, for the Atlanta Symphony Orchestra, completed a kind of informal trilogy of 'portraits of nature' as Glass saw them at the time, balancing the 'portrait opera' trilogy that he completed with *Akhnaten*, following *Einstein On The Beach* and *Satyagraha*, in 1983.

Symphonic in scope and even in approach these pieces may have been, but that was not enough for Davies. 'I'm not going to let you', he told Glass at the time, 'be one of those opera composers that never writes a symphony.' It sounds like a rashly optimistic assertion, because Glass himself did not much mind if he indeed turned out to be 'one of those opera composers'. After all, that is more or less how he saw himself and how he still sees himself. He is having to accept that his work adds up to something altogether broader, but left to himself he would never have made the time to let it happen. Davies's wish needed further years of patience, but it proved to be founded on an extraordinarily far-sighted judgment, a shrewd assessment of character and an accurate imaginative insight into the potential for a new body of work different from anything Glass had composed before. From 1992 onwards, the world began to find out why. Davies was right to believe that Glass would respond to commissions if the circumstances were suitable, and right to think that a series of Glass symphonies would build up into a substantial achievement. His faith and persistence were rewarded, as of early 2002, with six full-scale symphonies, all of which he either premièred or conducted early on, and all of which (bar the last, so far,) he has recorded:

PG: 'It just happened. People asked for pieces and I wrote them. I didn't really expect to write them. The main work has been on the operas and I did the symphonies in between things and I wasn't thinking about them very much, or the concertos. It's just that people asked for them. Almost all the concertos were commissioned by the players. All the concertos were written for people. The fact is that a lot of the time is spent writing operas and rehearsing operas.'

RM: 'All the same there is something happening as the line of symphonies develops, which is clear to anyone who follows symphonies. They evolve from one to another.'

PG: 'Do you think so? They do, in a way, don't they. If you find that from two to three, I think you will find it with five to six. I got interested in the way symphonies as a form evolved through the 20th century, and those symphonies by Shostakovich where text becomes involved so that the symphony became a very open form at that point. It wasn't any longer defined either by the romantic symphony or the classical, but by people who were really thinking about symphonies in a much grander way. That interested me more because once text got involved, then I had one foot back in the theatre world, I was in a world that was very familiar to me. Setting text with orchestras, that you do all the time. Singers with orchestras is something I know how to do very well.

'I was also more interested in pieces that had particular subject matter. Concert music doesn't really have subject matter except the language of music itself, whereas theatre music always has that. That's why I think that composers either gravitate one way or the other. For me the main thing was theatre music and then the symphonies were done in between. There's a good reason why a lot of symphonists never wrote operas. Brahms didn't, Beethoven wrote one then the Schubert ones are never done. It's a different way of thinking about music. I managed eventually to form some ideas about symphonies, but it's just because I wrote enough of them. I didn't set out to do it at all. They always happen when somebody asks for one, they won't happen otherwise. With operas I always have an idea of an opera I want to do, and I have to find someone to do it. Theatre work is usually motivated by my idea and then I have to organize the production. Symphonies are somebody else's idea and they organize the production.

'I don't think that has to do very much with the quality. I think they're good ones, I think they are OK, I think that they have something to say in a way. Those things become irrelevant. In the end the motivation isn't that important, it's what you end up with that's important.'

RM: 'That happens with opera composers too – look at Verdi who wrote all those early pieces, some of which are brilliant, because he had to write them, because that was his living.'

73

PG: 'That's the simple truth. I put off the timpani concerto for about ten years because I just couldn't imagine how I would do it, and Jonathan Haas was so persistent that I finally did it. He was a complete nuisance until I wrote it. I created all kinds of obstacles for him and he just surmounted them all. In the end, he found the performances.'

You would not guess Glass's attitude to approaching such work from listening to the completed music in question. That includes the timpani concerto, which manages to sound as if its composer thoroughly enjoyed himself while writing it, or at least it has a character that comes across in performances of revelling in its own flamboyant display:

PG: 'I've learnt that whether I want to do a piece or do not want to do a piece has very little to do with how the piece turns out. Once I start writing, something else comes into play, and so whether I wanted to write it or not becomes not so important. I never would have written the timpani concerto and it's a very popular piece. And it sounds like I enjoyed it. The origins of the pieces are biographical information, which is curious but irrelevant to the work itself. Finally you have to look at the music and see what the music does. What people may say about it may have very little to do with it.'

He may not want to do it, but he still does.

RM: 'Why do you take on the symphonic commissions? What makes you do it when you are so busy?'

PG: 'First of all Dennis [Russell Davies] wants them. He plays them and he records them, and he's been a great partner in getting the work done. He does the operas too. I'm not uninterested, it's just that you have to remember that when you write operas you're really working with symphonic material all the time. About eight of the operas use full orchestras. I have spent a lot of time with symphonic ensembles where you get five or six days of rehearsal. Not the usual few hours that a modern piece gets but five or six days, so there is a lot of time to think about the orchestra and learn about it, and along the way I've picked up a lot of techniques for working with that large ensemble. When I write a symphony then I'm not longer thinking about a theatrical subject. So it's like that.

'Then there's another thing too. At a certain point the whole enterprise gains a certain momentum. After six symphonies I'm starting to think, I wonder what seven will be like. The way it evolved, you're thinking of about 15 big orchestra pieces, and at a certain point it starts to command a kind of attention of its own, not in spite of me but regardless of me. It's there. Then people begin to like them. A conductor in California played *Symphony No 5* and he said he'd like to commission a new symphony. Then someone in Paris, one of the orchestras in Paris, said they would like a symphony. It's not with me. Now the *Symphony No 7* seems kind of inevitable, whereas it never would have seemed to me like that before.

'That kind of momentum, it didn't happen before I got to four or five, the first two or three or four I didn't think about that much, but with five and six now it's taken a certain direction and I've become curious about what it might take. Now that I've had the large vocal ensemble of *Symphony No 5* and the solo voice of *Symphony No 6* I can easily imagine continuing in this vein with vocal elements in it. But at a certain point it might be interesting also to go back and do a purely instrumental work. I think I'll need to do a few other pieces first.'

So much for the future...meanwhile the six symphonies that may continue to a seventh or an eighth, another vocal piece or another instrumental one, have their own story to tell. They fall into two distinct groups, not on the instrumental-or-vocal criterion but because of their content. It is also a chronological division. The first three are as it happens just for orchestra, two for full symphony orchestra and the third for a smaller group of strings, and what they have in common is a conventional sequence of movements and a consistently developing kind of musical thought. From *No 4* there is a change: the forms are more individual, the structures quite different from one to the next and the work takes on a cross-art form, extra-musical dimension whether that is theatrical, philosophical or poetic – arguably all three in the case of *No 6*, as will be seen.

The first of them had a typically quirky set of origins. It sprang not only from Dennis Russell Davies' heroic persistence but from a striking and altogether more worldly circumstance: the economics of a record company. In the early 1990s Glass and the then Polygram company founded a label called Point Music. It lasted about ten years on a basis of mutual interest. In outline, the deal was that Glass would be able to get music recorded that he liked but that might not sell many copies, in return for the label also issuing music he liked that would sell. As part of that commitment he thought he could write something to give it a boost. So there was a down-to-earth motivation at work. No mystique about that: to borrow a turn of phrase that Glass likes to use in situations where convoluted or evasive attitudes are the norm among serious composers, 'it's very simple'. Brahms wrote his first symphony quite late in life because he had agonized for decades over the responsibility of contributing to the form that Beethoven had turned into a vehicle for great and profound thoughts. Glass had not got round to it before because nobody had asked him.

Even so, not everybody would put forward their first symphony as a way of improving a commercial company's fortunes. The idea Glass had was ingenious. It was to base a composition of his own on the classic album *Low* by David Bowie and Brian Eno, released in 1977. On the surface it looks like a recipe for making incompatible worlds collide. Progressive pop and progressive classical music have traditionally inhabited different aesthetic universes and appealed to mutually exclusive groups of people, each likely to regard their own choice as an escape from the other. There was more to it than that, and more too than being able to put the names of Bowie, and to some extent Eno, on a classical album in order to attract buyers who would not otherwise touch it – a circumstance of which Glass, long accustomed to dealing with the commercial music world, would nevertheless be well aware. The music does not have to sound like Bowie or Eno to create an immediate level of interest before a note has been heard. A good marketing move, then.

If that were all, the name of *Low Symphony* would just be an exercise in cynical opportunism, whereas the connections run rather deeper. They have more to do with the nature of 1970s pop than with

Glass's music in the 1990s. The original *Low* album came out towards the end of a period of around ten years in which some of the more experimental and original spirits in pop were listening to new music from classical sources that ranged from the Stockhausen end of the spectrum through to the American minimalists. The *Low Symphony* was written near the beginning of another phase in pop and dance music, in which the newly accessible skills of digitally manipulating musical sounds and phrases would produce something of a creative explosion. Eno was an essential link between these two movements, pioneering a powerful range of studio techniques and ambient styles when the technology was still hard to get to grips with and continuing to experiment up to the present day. His own formative influences included the experimental genres of the 1960s and 1970s and the minimalists too. They are part of the collaboration with Bowie along with the rock tradition and Bowie's personal songwriting style. There already was a link, then, whether Glass happened to be interested or not. It was becoming part of the common culture of the Anglo-American world.

Glass had never tried to write pop music and he was not going to start now. At the same time he has always kept in touch with cultural currents beyond the self-contained environment of classical music. What he did was entirely in keeping with his ways of working in theatre or film, at least in its origins. He looked for ways of working with other people's material that allowed him to compose his own music without compromise. He decided to take themes from three of the instrumental numbers on *Low* and use them as part of an extended work. It took the form of a symphony because the opportunity was there for an orchestra to commission and perform it, and a recording could therefore be made easily. That opportunity was secured by Dennis Russell Davies, this time by way of another of his New York connections, the Brooklyn Philharmonic Orchestra, which offered the commission. The honour of the first public performance in Munich on 30 August 1992 went to a young musicians' orchestra with which Davies was working, the Junge Deutsche Kammerphilharmonie. But the Brooklyn players made the recording.

It has to be said that Bowie fans who went for the music on the strength of its title were in for a bewildering experience. The symphony had a hostile reception from pop reviewers who complained that it had none of the spirit of rock music and found it plain dull. A few listeners from the pop area no doubt found it opened their ears to a range of contemporary music they had been unaware of, and will have been grateful ever after, but self-conscious education work or missionary posturing was not the purpose of the piece. When people liked the music, the reason was straightforward. The outstanding feature of the *Low Symphony* is that it is pure Glass from start to finish. The themes from Bowie and Eno take their place alongside other inventions of Glass's own and, as Glass has written, were deliberately treated as though they too were Glass's own. There is not a moment of pastiche or imitation. You can go further than that, because unless you know the original album you can listen to the entire 40-minute work unaware that anybody else's themes were involved. This is more like the time-honoured way that classical composers have written variations and fantasies in their own style on other people's tunes, with the added twist that even the tunes wear the composer's own clothing.

The music follows a quite different path from classical variation form but the principle is the same.

Classical critics too did not like the *Low Symphony*, but that is a situation that crops up again and again with his work. By 1992 two constituencies of rejection had sprung up. The older one included those who stood for a previous generation's view of contemporary music, never liked the minimalists to start with and had no time for anything the composers did afterwards. The more recent consisted of people who became hooked on the early pieces and found it hard to accept the way in which Glass had moved on. This is a no-win situation that does not seem to have troubled the broader musical public, though in some places it affected their chances of hearing the symphonies in concert – in London, a world musical centre by any criterion, it was not until the 2001/02 season that all the instrumental symphonies were played, and the remaining two still have no performances planned.

All this aside, as first symphonies go the *Low Symphony* is an unusually confident one. It springs directly out of the extended orchestral forms of *The Light* (see pp.46–7) and the *Violin Concerto*. Glass, while saying that he allowed the transformations of the themes 'to follow my own compositional bent when possible', reckoned that the music of Bowie and Eno had an influence on the way he worked, leading him to 'sometimes surprising musical conclusions', so that he arrived at 'something of a real collaboration between my music and theirs'. Ten years on, when the main surprise is still that the piece is a symphony at all, the sense of collaboration is not something you would wish to pin down by hard-and-fast musical analysis, except for the obvious: there are points where the musical ideas are by Bowie/Eno and the orchestration and arrangement are by Glass. Otherwise there is the primary level of the way one musical mind and set of instincts has responded to themes that sprang from another. It is about qualities such as colour and mood. The score has a distinctive, lean and transparent sound of its own that stands apart from the more saturated and brilliant orchestral sound of *The Light* and of the next symphony. When there is a parallel to the album, however, it is translation rather than imitation. Mostly, trying to link up symphony and album while listening is a tempting waste of time. Just as films based on novels are more directly experienced if you have never read the book, so this symphony is best approached on its own terms.

For the record, the first movement is named for Bowie's track 'Subterraneans', the remaining two for Bowie/Eno tracks: 'Some Are' and 'Warszawa' (the latter should also be credited as itself borrowing a Polish traditional song). The direct translations into Glass's language are placed at the outset of each. Then the music does what it has to do. What you hear is a long, initially steady-paced prelude, which eventually picks up speed; then a kind of classical scherzo composed on Glass's terms; and a sombre finale with moments of more energetic contrast. If you are looking for precedents the horn lines near the beginning will remind you more of Copland than of anything in the rock archives, but the Glass fingerprints are all over it: oscillating woodwind, pulsing strings, an obsessive bass and trumpets leading a shapely melodic extension. The music develops in its own way, exploring the implications of an idea as it occurs, until another of the ideas it has alternated with takes the lead; new ideas drop in, older ones drop out for a while. These are the elements of Glass's personal symphonic technique, practised in the overtly dramatic situations of stage works and orchestral 'portraits', and to some extent in the string quartets but in miniature, and now having their muscles flexed at length. The result is a long build towards a single emphatic peak right at the end, staying quiet much of the way, turning to darker orchestral colours in passing and stepping up the pace in stages.

A light orchestral touch also figures in the scherzo movement. Descending scales and swaying chords clash, reconcile their differences, briefly peak and then go their own ways as a violin line takes over: slightly dark in tone but genuinely playful. At the centre there is an obvious break for what sounds like the 'Trio' section of the 19th-century classical scherzos – even more so since it features a clarinet line that seems like updated Schubert, later transferring meltingly to strings. There is a revised revisit to the earlier material, plus a new repeating arpeggio-based figure that combines with the swaying chords – a very characteristic Glass figure and, as it will prove, a characteristic time, close to the end of a movement, for launching a new idea. The finale sets out with a slow pulse, bleak high chords and quietly menacing brass. A melody growls up from the lower strings. In a more relaxed section recurring descents in high strings take turns with further inspections and developments of the same melody, which grow into the dominating feature of the movement as they sing out in the violins. They are joined by patterns of quiet brass chords and oscillating accompaniments, which towards the end break out into more assertive semiquavers as the melodic elements rearrange themselves until string descents, brass chords and calm oscillations succinctly fade the music out.

In an often understated way, this music provides plenty of information about Glass's symphonic language. It uses figures that have featured in Glass's music since the beginning – quick repeating groups of six or eight notes, based on arpeggios and broken chords; pulses and oscillations; patterns that gradually extend – and adds the kinds of short, striking sequences of chords that he began to use from the time of *Einstein On The Beach*. But they are arranged in different ways and joined by other elements that came into his music when he began composing for the opera house: melody (outstandingly) and the use of orchestral colour to characterize themes or blocks of music. And it is these elements that determine the different ways of arranging and structuring the music. In Glass's minimalist days rhythm was the main, and sometimes the only, structural principle. Now rhythm is one among others. Themes and ideas are characterized by rhythm as well as colour. They alternate, extend and give way to new ideas. In this way, while the music is kept in shape by rhythm, its growth is determined by melody and the interaction between musical ideas.

It is music that develops symphonically as it goes along. This distinguishes it from more traditional symphonic forms that tend to separate the statement of themes from their development. In one sense it goes back to first classical principles in that Haydn, and to a lesser extent Mozart, would often appear to develop ideas as they thought of them; but they still liked to have a middle section of deliberate development and harmonic wandering, and the successors who formed the 19th-century tradition put the emphasis firmly on that section. Sure enough there are reprises and revisits to earlier material in the later part of a Glass symphonic movement, but these are woven into the ongoing continuum rather than being placed as a return home after discursive wanderings. Discussion is something that can happen as soon as the ideas appear; it is not hived off into a separate section. A further consequence is that, as we have already seen, new material can join the music right up to the final stages.

There is another good reason for this kind of structuring. Glass's music may be consonant, based in particular keys and rooted in classical harmonic sequences, but it is not actively, dynamically tonal in the same sense as a classical symphony. In music from Beethoven through to Mahler and beyond, events such as the movement away from the home key and its eventual return could be made into moments of burgeoning adventure and high drama. In some early 20th-century pieces, by Mahler again and independently by the Danish symphonist Carl Nielsen, the symphony could actually move dramatically from one key at the start to another at the end. The organizing principles that Glass uses take the place of classical and romantic composers' long-range changes of key and the build-ups of tension that spring from them. There are key changes over time, but they are not the very basis of the music as they are in, say, the symphonies of Beethoven, Brahms or Bruckner. Keys may also clash in the bitonal sense of one harmony superimposed on another – like the relationship of melody and accompaniment at the start of the *Low Symphony*'s middle movement – but this is harmonic colour rather than tonal tension. The absence of prominent tonal tension is one of the key features of Glass's music at all times; it contributes to an apparently mysterious quality of long-term serenity no matter how intense events may become on the surface or from moment to moment. As many composers before Glass have found, if you downgrade tonality you lose the essential organizing element of classical and romantic symphonic form. This is why the surviving 20th-century symphonists remained essentially tonal composers in the traditional sense, and even the apparently atonal Maxwell Davies harked back to Sibelius. It is also why Schoenberg and Berg did not write symphonies, while Webern once used the term but for music on a much smaller scale. If you are going to go the whole hog, you have to reinvent the form.

Two years later the Brooklyn Philharmonic and Dennis Russell Davies were at it again. The *Symphony No 2* followed the *Low Symphony* into the world on 15 October 1994, commissioned by the Brooklyn Academy of Music, and this time the orchestra got to play the première. (Not the recording, though, which was done two years later at another of Davies's regular haunts, the studios of Austrian Broadcasting, by the Vienna Radio Symphony Orchestra.) It follows on in more substantial ways, too, with three movements running altogether for about the same length as its predecessor, and a similar personal approach to building its material into an extended form.

Oscillations and pulses, then over them a rather plain and sometimes harmonically clashing melody, are the initial elements from which the music grows in colour, scale and range, taking in an archetypal sequence of four chords. Once again the music starts to vary and develop itself straight away, without waiting for all the new material to be presented. The melody may be plain but it is potent, with its alternately rising and falling phrases – the latter coming to be dominant. At the centre the pace moves up a gear as the first theme renews its transformations, dropping back again for the final stages. Another movement then grows out of it as if the music were continuous: same harmony, even the same undulating string pattern. The pace is exactly the same as the opening of the symphony though without the lift in the rhythm, but when the woodwind join the texture it is with another extension of the first movement's rising phrase. Pulsing brass send the music off on a course of its own, featuring more abrupt fluctuations of speed and power before another gentle subsidence.

Then, surprise: the finale kicks in with a rapid but austere burst of music for all the world like an orchestral encounter with Glass's past – specifically the figurations of the minimalist pieces from the early days of the Philip Glass Ensemble. It does not stay around for enough time to start extending itself to the great lengths of old. On the contrary it is one block of music among several that alternate and interact, most of them in character with the rest of the symphony and continuing to expand on what proves to have been its fundamental melodic phrase. Towards the end an exuberant momentum develops, enlivened by diverting chromatic slithers and moving towards the sizzling energy of another Philip Glass Ensemble incarnation, the touring group of the later 1970s, all the while flexing its muscles with the freedom of Glass's current inventive power. For the first time in his symphonies, and so far the only time although it became a recurrent feature in concertos, a musical feel-good factor had emerged to take over and dominate the final stages.

Despite this vivid conclusion, the symphony is less captivating an experience than its predecessor. The long middle section of the first movement extends its material in a relentlessly un-virtuoso way that certainly maintains its expansive proportions but at the expense of immediate variety and colour. The main melody of the work is not one of Glass's more sensuous or affecting inventions. Instead the music is more about its own inner workings, handled with intricate attention, technical aplomb and, for all its length, economy of means. But the upshot is that it feels a transitional work, something that Glass may have needed to do to develop his own prowess in the genre. The feeling is rather confirmed when the next symphony, premièred just a few months later, sets out on a completely different tack.

Symphony No 3 was commissioned for the Stuttgart Chamber Orchestra and first performed, with Dennis Russell Davies conducting, on 5 February 1995. The same performers recorded it 20 months later. It is written for string orchestra alone, and specifically for 19 players all of whom have their own part at different stages of the work. This gives it a certain kinship with the string-quartet medium, and at around 24 minutes – just over half the length of the first two symphonies – the work is also closer to Glass's quartets in length. But it sounds like another symphony on the model that Glass had established, only more tightly worked.

Its economy of means is clear from the start, and also its symphonic nature. If you compare the opening with the beginning of the fifth quartet's second movement (which follows a brief prelude), you hear paragraphs of similar quiet pulsing music but a difference of scale. The quartet is already on to its second movement, and this sounds from context and working as if it is going to be another relative miniature – quite correctly. The symphony in contrast plunges straight into music about as elemental as music can be: just the note C, pulsing steadily in different registers: bass line on the beat, top line syncopated. Classical symphonies could have elemental beginnings too – think of Beethoven's *Ninth*, and nearly all Bruckner's symphonies – but what ensues in them is a musical structure that uses well established rules. The start of Glass's *No 3* is like reducing the elements of a classical symphony down to absolute fundamentals, as a preparation for building again from scratch. If that sounds a familiar ploy, it is because Glass has done it before, only with the whole language of music, back in the 1960s when he abandoned the style he had learnt in favour of the elemental rhythm-based processes of his minimalist days. This time what he has done is not a devastating overhaul of past practice: it is founded on a now well-established and constantly enlarging musical language. But the opening has the same immediate, cleansing effect.

Soon afterwards, the musical lines start wandering – not within the key of C, like a classical symphony, or even into related keys, but straight away into scales that clash with it. The pulsing Cs continue and, even when the wandering lines become longer and more animated, they are always there, if not actually sounding then quick to return. In itself this is quite a short movement but it appears to be setting up something longer, and it runs straight into the next with an abrupt increase of speed and change of texture. Strings in octaves power through a vigorous passage in even quavers with an 18-quaver rhythmic cycle – its divisions are 5/4/4/5 – and a similar tendency to wander off chromatically. Harmony creeps in and more strings are added as the flow continues until the cycle expands to 23 quavers and a quick-change accompaniment of plucked chords underpins it. This music reaches a dynamic peak and then suddenly gives way to a new, and as it turns out concluding, section: lightly plucked strings joined by a fragment of melody on the violas, which extends to the violins and dies away on the basses.

Melody is the essence of the next movement, which is the symphony's expansive heart. It takes time to realise that, because initially the music reverts to quiet beats and familiar (in a Glass context) oscillating lines. Add pulsing chords, and gradually more layers, and the music reveals itself as a steady build-up of density over a recurring harmonic pattern, longer than the short sequences of the chaconne form, which is its nearest classical precedent. It is static, in a tonal sense, and it amasses a quiet grandeur. Melody eventually arrives with a solo violin, and it is an extensive, luscious melody that floats over the harmonic pattern. Still this is not all: further decorative violin lines, trills and filigrees, play above the melody as it repeats. The effect is like a single image of beauty assembled piece by piece until it achieves its full intensity. The image appears to be frozen in time and has a deeply affecting impact on a live audience. When it is fully achieved there is no lingering, it just gives way immediately to resumed running quavers in octaves at exactly the same speed as the second movement. And it is resuming unfinished business in more than one sense: this opening of the finale is a variation of the 'new' theme from the end of the second movement, in the manner of that movement's beginning. Short and pointed, the finale brings in explicit quotations from earlier and a flurry of chromatic scales before the briefest of conclusions, a sudden drop back to quiet sustained harmony and an elemental pulse.

Detail like this shows why this symphony is one of Glass's most all-of-a-piece, tautly unified works. In one sense it also turned out to be the end of a line. Having distilled his symphonic thinking up to this point into a subtly absorbing form, where else was there to go? The answer would be, back to familiar ground in the theatre and the human voice. But the slow movement proved to be a precedent. His *Violin Concerto* had featured an expansive and melodically haunting slow movement, but this was the first time music of such direct and frank expression had appeared in one of his symphonies. It helps to set the tone of the long lyrical upsurges that would appear at the heart of two later concertos, those for piano and for cello. It also sets a technical precedent, for the massive repeating sequences that would bring his *Symphony No 6* to its devastating peak. Before that, there came one more purely instrumental work, which was already the beginning of the next phase.

One year on again, Glass had decided on one aspect of the next symphony before he knew about any dance connection. It was to return to the sources of his first. The *Heroes Symphony* springs from material in another Bowie/Eno album from the 1970s: a follow-up to a follow-up, then, and also to be issued on Point Music. He happened to mention the project to the American choreographer Twyla Tharp, and Tharp immediately became excited at the prospect of making dance to it. She went and listened to the original *Heroes* album, and a meeting was set up between Tharp, Glass and Bowie at which the plan was agreed. Bowie had given his blessing to the *Low Symphony* and liked the results, so he was pleased. As for Glass, he said, 'I found myself writing a symphonic score that was shortly to become a ballet.'

The choreographed *Heroes* proved to be the first public airing of the music, presented in September 1996 as the final part of a Tharp touring triple bill called, unambiguously, 'Tharp!' A hugely experienced and respected pioneer in her field, Tharp had formed a new young company for this tour, and the programme was by all accounts a brilliant and absorbing experience. The dance work explored what, in an American and also an East German context (the latter reflecting aspects of the Bowie album), the notion of a hero might mean but, as with all of her choreography, it was a dazzling exploration of the elements and nature of dance itself. The tour ran through the following season and went to Europe during the summer. By this time, the score had already been heard in concert. Dennis Russell Davies had set up a performance with the Vienna Radio Symphony Orchestra on 5 June 1997, but he was narrowly beaten to the world concert première by an enterprising festival in the northern suburbs of London. It was 15 May 1997 when the Crouch End Festival heard *Heroes* played by the leading British chamber orchestra, the Academy of St Martin in the Fields, conducted by Martyn Brabbins. Glass had shown up for the festival and on the next day he gave a concert with the Philip Glass Ensemble, which included a version of extracts from the *Low Symphony* as well as music from the first operatic trilogy and another early stage work, *The Photographer*. Davies's recording, which came out the same year, was made with the American Composers Orchestra.

Heroes is different from any of the preceding symphonies. It falls into six quite concise movements, each springing from a track on the album: 'Heroes', 'Abdulmajid', 'Sense Of Doubt', 'Sons Of The Silent

Age', 'Neukoln', 'V2 Schneider'. Once again the elements of the original are translated into Glass's own terms. At the opening you can, if you fancy, hear a kind of squeezed-out riff with the tune floated over it, but soon the music is off on its own track of characteristic chord patterns and scales. This time the forms are simpler, often using a contrasting middle section and a straightforward or varied return to the opening material. The most symphonic, in Glass's previous terms, is the last movement, where a complex alternation of themes and figures takes on new ideas as it goes along, and builds up momentum to a buoyant close. Otherwise the main principle of contrast is colour and pace. 'Abdulmajid's tune comes dangerously close to exoticism but it is given a lean, laconic and eventually poetic treatment. 'Sons Of The Silent Age' actually starts like a rather easy-going, reharmonized pop song, before going Glass's way. Most haunting and evocative are 'Sense Of Doubt' and the quite stark 'Neukoln'.

Perhaps the 'collaboration' that Glass reckoned to have taken place with *Low* was a little nearer the mark this time. It is not that Bowie had any direct input to the score, but he did say afterwards that 'Philip's actually put his finger on more of my original voice...very near to the gut feeling of what I was trying to do.' Be that as it may, people who wanted a literal re-creation of the Bowie album in orchestral guise will again have been disappointed, although they did have a more upbeat, succinct and vigorous piece to listen to. More to the point, in the symphonic context, is that it marked the appearance of theatrical considerations: *Heroes* feels like a dance symphony, just as it would feel like a symphonic song cycle if it had vocal parts. Almost immediately, the opportunity to bring voices into a symphony on the very largest scale was to move this second phase of Glass's symphonic career into another dimension again.

Just before the *Symphony No 5* had its West Coast première in October 2000, Glass was telling the audience of a public talk how the music came about. It was a sponsored commission by the Salzburg Festival in the year before the new millennium began. In the process of setting up the commission, in 1997, he went to a meeting where he learned that the multi-national sponsoring company, American Standard Code for Information Interchange (ASCII) Corporation, wanted to mark the significance of the transition from 1999 to 2000 with 'a piece like Beethoven's *Ninth*'. The transcript of the talk then reads: 'I said... "Sure".' No composer is rash enough to think he or she can deliver a piece of any quality 'like Beethoven's *Ninth*' to order, and Glass's reply has to go down as one of the great laconic deadpan statements of musical history. (Were it not for the honour of the commission and the stature of the festival, it must have been tempting for him to come back with 'well why don't you play Beethoven's *Ninth*?') Nevertheless, the sponsors got their choral symphony from Glass. The festival wanted the new millennium marked. Glass took the context and its implications seriously, and decided that if there were to be a guarantee of momentousness it would have to be provided by a text. That sounds modest, but it was really a matter of calling on his personal experience and approach to music. So far he did not see his symphonies as doing anything momentous, rather as being thrown off between operas, while his main energies in recent years had gone into composing with texts that he had had the main say in selecting or setting up.

The question was, what text? Specially written for the occasion, or of already proven stature? He thought that this time it should be a kind of anthology. He also wanted it to have what amounted to a religious dimension, in so far as it would consist of writings from what he has called 'wisdom' traditions. Personally a Buddhist, he decided that the work should have a wider range of perspectives than his own, and he took on collaborators to help suggest and research sources. They were the Very Rev James Parks Morton, president of the Interfaith Center of New York, and Kusumilla Priscilla Pedersen, chair of the department of religious studies at St Francis College, Brooklyn Heights. What the three of them came up with was 'a compendium of reflection on the process of global transformation and evolution' in the words of classic texts from across the world. The sequence began with creation and pre-creation myths, ranged across fundamental experiences of life and death and passed through apocalyptic dreams to visions of paradise and a dedication to the future; timeless, then, rather than a self-conscious attempt at contemporary statement or an assembly of too-specific moments from history. Also fallible in that it involved choices, and therefore omissions, made by human beings; but because of that personal, and capable of being understood as a work of art rather than an act of devotion. The plan falls into three sections, which correspond to the three phrases of the sequence just outlined. Each section consists in turn of four movements, and most of the movements have several sources. In the past Glass has often used texts in ancient languages, but for the symphony all the words were taken in English translation to emphasize what the traditions might share – that there could be unity as well as difference within their diversity.

These are the 12 movements of the symphony, as well as details of their literary sources and their original languages:

I   'Before The Creation': the *Rig Veda* (Sanskrit)

II   'Creation Of The Cosmos': the *Koran* (Arabic), *Genesis* (Hebrew), the *Kumulipo* (Hawaiian), *Zuni Creation Story* (Zuni)

III 'Creation Of Sentient Beings': the *Nihongi* (Japanese), the *Kumulipo*, *Bulu Creation Story* (Bulu), *Boshongo Creation Story* (Bantu)

IV   'Creation Of Human Beings': the *Popul Vuh* (Quiche Maya), the *Koran*

V   'Love And Joy': *Rumi* (Persian), the *Song Of Songs* (Hebrew), *Vidyapati* (Bengali), *Jagadananda-dasa* (Bengali)

VI   'Evil And Ignorance': the *Popul Vuh*, the *Maha-Vagga* (Pali), *Bhagavad Gita* (Sanskrit)

VII 'Suffering': *Psalms* (Hebrew), *Bhagavad Gita, Job* (Hebrew), *Hosea* (Hebrew)

VIII 'Compassion': *Mencius* (Chinese), *Bodhicaryavatara* (Sanskrit), *Matthew* (Greek)

IX   'Death': the *Sought-for Grave* (Japanese), *Ono No Komachi* (Japanese), *Haiku* by Matsuo Basho (Japanese), *Bodhicaryavatara*

X   'Judgment And Apocalypse': the *Koran*, the *Tibetan Book Of The Dead* (Tibetan), the *Vishnu Purana* (Sanskrit)

XI   'Paradise': *Rumi, I Corinthians* (Greek), *Kabir* (Hindi)

XII 'Dedication Of Merit': *Bodhicaryavatara* (Sanskrit)

Can this really be a symphony? Glass was perfectly clear about it, calling it a symphony to stress that it was a secular concert work. All

95

the same, it is certainly personal. It carries the title 'Requiem, Bardo, Nirmanakaya', which certainly continues to mix the sources – Latin-Christian, Tibetan, Sanskrit – but has a certain Buddhist leaning. The three words together suggest a progression through and beyond death, though two of them will probably be unfamiliar to those who have not studied Buddhism. They have quite specific meanings. Bardo refers to an intermediate state, slightly comparable to the Christian purgatory, which exists after death and before (in Buddhist terms) rebirth, and during which it is possible for the person who has died to escape the death-rebirth circle and achieve enlightenment, if the person can recognize the true nature of reality. The extract from the *Tibetan Book of the Dead* in movement X relates to it. Nirmanakaya is the state of enlightened perfection, occupied by beings who renounce nirvana – spiritual bliss – and choose self-sacrifice. The text of the final movement comes out of that state, written in the first person as a series of wishes for the world and ending with the fervent wish, 'may I too abide to dispel the misery of the world'. All the texts, Glass has said, are compatible with Buddhism though they are mostly not Buddhist. Nevertheless they belong to a musical performance, not a devotional act. Up until the last stages of the work, the implication of the title is that the work has the character of a requiem, but the texts themselves ensure that it is a requiem in the broadest sense, a reflection on creation and life in the context of death, and by analogy on the content and close of a millennium, concluded in a spirit of hope for the life, and the millennium, to come. The words can be read and listened to as literature, without any technical knowledge of the traditions they belong to. In that sense the symphony is intended to be as universal as any art can be that originates within a specific culture.

This stage of the creative process, before he went away and composed the score, echoes the way Glass often works in the theatre, at least as far as the libretto of an opera is concerned – obviously there is no element of stage design or production. To that extent it impinges on the traditional concerns of opera and, just as much, oratorio – an artistic borderland that Glass has visited before in one of his first operas, *Satyagraha*, which he has called a choral opera and certainly works in concert performance. But, however closely opera and oratorio may relate to each other, what they have in common is essentially the element of drama. It does not have to be narrative drama – think of Handel's *Messiah*, a reflection on the life of Christ in which the main character does not even appear – but the experience is still dramatic. So is the experience of a classical symphony, with its vigorous interaction of tonalities and keys. But the drama there is an abstract one. Beyond that, the first four of Glass's symphonies have already redefined the form in a manner that works with his own musical language – even more abstract, if you like. The fifth has a text that is deliberately reflective rather than dramatic, and perfectly suited to music that will illustrate and respond in the course of finding its own form. Symphonic in its essentials, then, but once again taking the idea of what a symphony can be a stage further.

The music has dramatic moments, but it is overwhelmingly led and shaped by the words, with musical themes that are developed and reappear in a rather free symphonic format across the 12 movements. Colour, pace and dynamics – there are long stretches of quiet music that offset the expected grand sonorities – provide the main principles of contrast. Strikingly the choruses, one adult and one children's, sing in a consistent block-like way: almost all in rhythmic unison, mostly harmonized, sometimes in a single line. The very few occurrences of counterpoint are at moments that, in their different ways, call for extreme intensity. Lyrical expression is mostly the preserve of the vocal soloists and the orchestra. This polarizing of resources increases the monumental quality of the music, and emphasizes what one reviewer called the 'mosaic technique' of its construction.

Because of this the music in the long run has the effect of accumulating more than developing: nothing new in Glass, but different from the earlier symphonies and, in this respect at least, attuned to some of his operas. What it accumulates is powerful in its own right and contains music of characteristic beauty and rather more expressive eloquence than his purely instrumental symphonic writing. As often is the case with Glass the human voice, like the solo instrument in a concerto (and in the slow movement of the third symphony), releases an additional lyrical dimension. The première took place as one of the biggest events in the 1999 Salzburg Festival, on 31 August. Dennis Russell Davies conducted an assembly of European and American performers centred on the Vienna Radio Symphony Orchestra, with which he was to make the symphony's recording at the Austrian Broadcasting Studios the following spring.

Davies apart, the circumstances were different from most of Glass's first performances in its unusual degree of international prominence. Apart from a few of the operas, the prominence builds up gradually in most cases, as a result of tours, repeated performances around the world and recordings. This time the symphony was exposed to the full spectrum of reactions straight away – which is to say, because many of the attenders at Salzburg go for social as much as musical reasons, the habitual Glass-rejecters were out in force among the audience and the critics as well as the Glass-watchers. 'Bravos und Buhs fur eine Friedenssymphonie' ('Bravos and Boos for a peace symphony') was a fairly typical headline to an on-the-one-hand, on-the-other-hand review. 'Glass succombe au kitsch millenariste' ('Glass succumbs to millenium-inspired kitsch') was a little more extreme, though only to be expected. When the symphony had its US première just over a year later at the Brooklyn Academy of Music, the *New York Times* had it previewed by the usually sympathetic Allan Kozinn but sent to the performance another critic, the British diehard champion of modernism Paul Griffiths, who was to discover that 'the single interesting point…came right at the end'. By this he meant that the symphony went briefly into 'darker, more chromatic territory' before its emphatic conclusion, interpreting the passage as an undercutting of 'preposterous pretensions' and the arrival of an ironic dimension, rather than the straightforward variant of the symphony's opening (which itself had already been repeated at the start of the finale) that it consists of. Nothing new in that review, then. Listeners of this symphony just heard what they wanted to hear, as usual.

If musical irony were ever Glass's style at all, it is the raging and scathing kind rather than the self-referential. Something like you might find in the poems of Allen Ginsberg, for instance. Glass knew Ginsberg well, and had collaborated with him on the performance piece

Hydrogen Jukebox, which featured Ginsberg reciting as well as singers performing settings of his poems. They had wanted to make a successor work from Ginsberg's *Plutonian Ode*, a devastatingly angry and sustained assault on the effects of nuclear power, which he had written in 1978. The project remained unrealized when Ginsberg died in 1997, but the opportunity to make amends posthumously came about through a surprising piece of lateral thinking that sprang from Glass's next commission for a symphony. In 2002 Dennis Russell Davies was to reach the end of his final season as conductor of the American Composers Orchestra. The penultimate in a series of special events he organized through the season was a 65th birthday concert for Glass at the Carnegie Hall in New York. It was another opportunity to seek a new concert work from the reluctant provider. The upshot was a joint commission by Carnegie Hall and the Brucknerhaus in Linz, Austria, where Davies is music director of the Bruckner Orchestra: the symphony's second performance was due to open the 2002/03 season's Bruckner Festival.

Davies, an accomplished interpreter of Wagner as well as Bruckner, has drawn interesting parallels between Glass and Bruckner in their use of apparent accompanying figures as building blocks of symphonic music, their liking for repeated patterns and, naturally, their ability to write on an epic scale. It will have been interesting to see how the Austrian traditionalists took the *Symphony No 6*, because what they got was certainly 50 increasingly epic minutes, but they were minutes such as the concert hall had never heard from Glass before. He had remembered his 'unfinished business' with Ginsberg. Having set the project aside for some years, he was thinking of continuing with a version of *Plutonian Ode* for narrator and piano. But he eventually accepted that, since nobody else could recite Ginsberg's poems the way Ginsberg himself did, this format would unfortunately reinforce the sense of the poet's absence. On the other hand a setting for voice and orchestra might rise to the occasion. The chance presented itself, and *Plutonian Ode* became a symphony with solo soprano who, at the first performance on 3 February 2002, was Lauren Flanigan.

So after a dance symphony and a choral symphony, a song symphony? Not a bit of it. *No 6* is by some distance Glass's most powerful work for the concert hall. Its heightened emotions, its drama and eventual grandeur, are at times straight out of the opera house. The symphonic precedents are not so much Mahler's *Song Of The Earth*, which had been a role model for vocal symphonies right through the 20th century, as the wilder movements of the 13th and 14th symphonies by Shostakovich. This goes at least for the first two of the symphony's three movements, which follow the poem's division into three parts. The poem's response to nuclear pollution proceeds with high scorn through an account of the half-life of the radioactive element plutonium and its effects; then to the responsibility of people who live in the environment it has polluted, and finally to the particular responsibility of artists and creators. The mood moves from disgust and despair to urgency and, when it comes to the artists, a degree of hope.

The music also moves through a progression of states, though it becomes a different and complementary one. Out of the initial slow, quiet, dark string textures, the music gradually ascends to the first sung lines, a long vocal paragraph, which is followed by an increase of animation. The voice sets out again and a new theme joins the texture, until pounding percussion in a fast 29-beat cycle step up the intensity. This pace now keeps going as the voice soars and chordal figures appear, the dynamic level ebbing and flowing but tending to increase until a big orchestral tutti ascends to the movement's peak. It dies away on a sustained chord, and the succinct close takes in variants of the opening, a brief sung phrase repeated by the orchestra, and conclusive low minor chords, the last overlaid by a high major chord. The clash of major and minor, an extreme instance of Glass's bitonality, remains a feature of the music. The next movement is half the length but even more restless, the thrust of the poem underlined as the soprano, urgent and rarely lyrical, sings over extending and developing rhythms and quick-change chords. Once again there is a climax towards the end, a violent orchestral outburst and a sudden clash of superimposed chords, descending to an abrupt, quiet, unresolved break-off.

Now, after the high drama, something very different begins. The music simply oscillates between two notes. After nearly half a minute the pitch shifts, then back again. After a full minute the music wanders a little further, and back, and wanders, and returns again. The texture fills out a little and the process begins again. Two minutes on, layers of brass and the thump of a drum mark another cycle. The process continues over and over, with a funeral double drum-stroke and finally, after eight minutes, a fade, a loss of pulse and the entry of the voice. Slow progressions of chords accompany her, later a layer of violin arpeggios and then the original steady process begins again. The voice peaks at the close of one cycle. The next, and most powerfully scored, cycle uses double chordal attacks with double bell-strokes. This massive, sustained ritual begins to dissolve after some 16 minutes, fading and sinking to a low unison. And there is one arching, heartbreakingly eloquent phrase to sing before the music halts.

Like a vast death rite, the music is astonishingly conclusive. Yet it sets words of hope, and the overwhelming stasis and darkness of this finale are like a total acceptance of the worst in humanity and the world, as a prelude to working for something even a little better. Mourning before rebirth. The archive tape of the only performance so far closes with a silence, a crescendo of evidently heartfelt applause and obvious ovations for the composer. The latter was to be expected at a birthday celebration, but the response to such music is anything but celebratory. Premièred at a time of gloom in New York, just months after the destruction of the World Trade Center, it appears by coincidence to have caught a public mood, not the aggressive tub-thumping of the US government but a deeper sense of loss, the loss of what remained of American innocence, the belief that America might have grown up enough to become an integral part of the world instead of a force at odds with it. Be that as it may, the music tells its own story and it is one that at the time of writing has yet to get around, since few people have heard the symphony. Once the word is out, though, it will probably go something like this: Glass the symphonist has come of age with a work that will speak to the most resistant, and astonish those who always had faith. The drama of the stage works, and the still beauty of the smaller-scale ritual in the slow movement of the third symphony, have come together in a way that is as fresh and original as it is emotionally affecting. Expect it to become a concert fixture quickly.

Scene 4
Solo And Orchestra

PG: 'The *Violin Concerto* was written to be popular. Written to be liked. And it is. My father had died in 1971 and he was a great lover of violin concertos. I wrote the piece in 1987 thinking, let me write a piece that my father would have liked. Very straightforward. I knew what he liked. He loved the Mendelssohn concerto; he loved the great concertos, he loved them all – even the Paganini concertos, there's a couple of them he liked. I wrote the piece kind of for him. He was gone but it takes a little while when a parent has gone, and the listener for me was him. A very smart nice man who had no education in music whatsoever, but the kind of person who fills up concert halls. They're the people that keep the whole business going. I rather think I've succeeded, I think he would have liked it. I mean this is what I guess! So I'm pleased with it. It's popular, it's supposed to be – it's for my Dad.'

Philip Glass's orchestral music may have been dragged into the world as the result of persistent requests, or nagging, from Dennis Russell Davies, keener to conduct it than the composer was to write it. But as the story of the symphonies has shown, he has often found a personal motivation. Supporting the record label he had committed his energies to, completing unfinished business with the late Allen Ginsberg or seeking out an expression of fears and hopes at the end of a millennium that drew on the wider world's wisdom: the music begins with practical circumstances and tends to be taken over by larger concerns. The frank tribute that grew out of his first opportunity to write a mature piece for orchestral concerts reflects the influence that Ben Glass turned out to have been. As the final chapter of this book recounts, the family record retail business had a lot to do with Philip Glass's early musical experience. His father tended to bring home records that sold badly, such as string quartets and contemporary music, 'to see what was wrong with them'. (Asked whether he would have done this with the concerto, Glass replies, 'He might have!') Father and son got to listen to an unusual repertoire, and they both became fascinated.

With the hindsight of 15 years' worth of music in similar forms that followed on from it, the *Violin Concerto* takes on a pivotal role – in the literal sense of pivot. It is a work that changed significantly between project and completion. In advance it seemed set to be like a concert transfer of the well established Glass style of the 1980s: cycles and chord sequences and accompaniment figures the raw material, repeats and concise extensions the driving force, melody floated above. Before he composed it, Glass expected it to have five short movements, as though it were beginning where the string quartets left off. There were also expectations on the part of the proposed soloist, Paul Zukofsky, who had wanted, for as long as Davies, to persuade Glass that the orchestral medium would work for him. Zukofsky specifically asked for a slow, high finale. The music duly set out with the classic Glass elements of pulsing chords and arpeggios and accumulating sections. Then it started growing.

As he has said in the context of the symphonies, whatever the motivation, once work begins then the music has a way of taking over. It is like the experience of novelists who, as they get writing and round out the characters, find that the life of the people they created starts giving them surprises and takes the plot off in new directions. With two movements having expanded, Glass found his original plan going out of reach, unless the concerto were to be unfeasibly long. In came the improbably traditional three-movement plan, fast-slow-fast – 'by accident', as he later said – and along with it the format that, among other listeners, his father would have grown used to from the concertos of the classical repertoire. What of the finale that Zukofsky wanted? Glass's finale developed a quiet, slow ending, looking back to the earlier movements, and that seemed to satisfy everybody.

There was a further degree of back-and-forth referrals between Glass and Zukofsky, which resulted for instance in the pitch level of the first movement being raised so that it sounded better on the solo instrument. Of the final version he was still able to say, 'I'm more interested in my own sound than in the capability of particular orchestral instruments. It is tailored to my musical needs.' This is the sort of comment you would have expected from Glass at the time, given the two decades of radical composing reform that preceded the concerto. Now it seems, if not quite defensive, then at least protective. Understandably so: from a composer who had changed the face of instrumental ensemble music and the nature of opera, a mainstream concerto was the last thing anybody expected. Even the string quartets were quirky. Not that he cared what people thought, of course, but the work still had to be nurtured into life. And it proved to be the start of something. Having rediscovered the time-honoured format, he came back to it over and over, in symphonies and concertos alike.

Even when the symphonies started to go off in a different direction, the concertos continued along a similar line. What's more, they embraced some aspects of it more fully as they went on, and it is in this context that the *Violin Concerto* 'pivots' from one phase of his work into another. It still echoes the tightness of the earlier works, but it contains a flowering of qualities that would grow more powerful with time. The most notable instance is the slow movement. A straightforward Glass gesture opens it, oscillating lower strings with a punctuating tonic bass-note, all on the same minor chord – prelude music that might have occurred in any format he composed in, from solo piano to opera. The oscillation speeds up slightly, and the bass becomes a descending line played three times over beneath a repeating chord sequence, followed by a fourth phrase like a cadence. The violin enters quietly on an upbeat, and the four phrases are played again as it extends. They are to be played 13 times in all, straight off. The violin varies its line, the orchestral violins add another line and so the music continues to grow in density up to the eighth time, in which the horns take over one of the string lines. From then on the textures gradually lighten again and lose their animation, until in the final variation the orchestra is very quiet and the solo line almost still. Then the music simply stops, unresolved and without a single note of coda, just like it does in one of Glass's early process pieces.

Repeating sections like this have appeared in his operas since *Satyagraha*. You could say that they have appeared in opera since the quartet in Verdi's *Rigoletto*, although never so rigorously extended. You could even say that they go back to the principle of the chaconne with variations, familiar in Baroque instrumental music (such as the *D Minor Partita* by J S Bach for solo violin), used occasionally in opera of the same period ('When I am laid in earth', from *Dido And Aeneas* by Purcell), and adopted for symphonic purposes by Brahms in the fourth movement of his *Symphony No 4* (in which, as a composer of the romantic age might well, he felt he had to add a freely modulating epilogue to give the music the conclusive power of a finale as he saw it). All the same, what Glass does feels new, because such frankly expressive lines never featured in his purely instrumental music in this way: some of the filigrees of the solo part recall the seamless lines of Bach.

On the other hand, more than anything else in the concerto it has the effect of linking the music to his theatre works with orchestra. But it turned out to be the start of something, instead of the culmination. Or rather two things. One we have already seen: it goes through the slow movement of the third symphony to the finale of the sixth, with their different and more elaborate takes on a similar principle of repeating sections. The second is the highly expressive nature of the melodic material in later concertos. For all the affecting beauty of this movement, once you know what followed over a decade later, it takes on the character of a first venture into the unknown, one that released a new power and confidence of which the fulfilment remained in the future.

What came meanwhile in the concerto line was something different again. Eight years on, the persistence of performing artists once again drew out of Glass a work that would never have so much as occurred to him if he had been left to himself. This time even the solo line-up is unlikely: a quartet of saxophones. The catalysts were the Rascher Saxophone Quartet, a long-established group formed in 1969 by the veteran European player Sigurd Rascher and currently led by his daughter Carina. The group had it commissioned by a consortium of European orchestras – from Swedish Radio, Liverpool, Dortmund and Belgium – and the Schleswig-Holstein Festival, which introduced it on 27 July 1995. Naturally the work soon found its way to the Stuttgart Chamber Orchestra and Dennis Russell Davies, who made the recording the following year. In the meantime the Rascher players had launched it on a wider international circuit, which saw it performed with over 30 orchestras in Europe and America by 1997.

The facts are only the start of the surprises, because the music sounds unlike anything else of Glass's, increasingly so as it goes on. It has a concise shape, a lightness of timbre, a wry and sometimes perky tone and a liking for timbres that range from biting to pastel. In fact it starts to sound positively French, and stretches of the last two of its four movements do not sound immediately as though they are Glass's at all – a unique situation for a composer who is often instantly recognizable. They could almost come out of something by Darius Milhaud or even, in the slow movement, one of the more reflective offerings of the quirky French composer Jean Françaix. Once again the music takes on a life of its own.

As usual it starts out quite typically, with a repeating phrase and a repeating melodic extension. Much of the first movement alternates and recycles characteristic chunks of music, but it remains quiet, shadowy and quick-changing, with a rather wistful moderato feeling. While each movement nominally gives prominence to a different member of the quartet, in practice the writing for the quartet is well varied throughout from suave chords through to the chains of descending scales that lead to this opening movement's final, unusual major-key resolution.

With the fast, squirming, low-lying line and syncopated chords of the scherzo that follows, the concerto moves into more unfamiliar zones, still light and restless, but rhythmically irregular and bitonally flavoured – this last a common trait in Glass's music during the 1990s but rarely in such a pacy and astringent context. The longest movement, still only eight minutes, comes third and sets out from an ambiguous sequence of regularly pulsing chords – nothing new about the ambiguity, but the length of the sequence and the prominent augmented harmony lend the music a fresh twist that, once the initial repetitions give way to freer developments, effectively disguises its composer's identity. Whoever said Glass was predictable? The little solo phrases on alto and soprano saxes, the duets between saxes and with orchestral woodwind and the striking colour of the baritone sax playing in octaves with a glockenspiel, have a playful as well as a gently melancholy character. Towards the end some more typical pulsing chords based on quiet and rather fat-toned brass remind us where we are until the music winds down with pauses and short rests to a wait-for-it chord.

What this sets up is another fizzy syncopated line with a fast blues colouring and a short finale, which slips in new themes between extensions of the first, notably one in parallel lines, which reflects one of the opening movement's ideas. A descent in chords by the quartet sets up a solo interlude, and when the orchestra slyly works its way back in it takes a fresh look at the material before familiar chords and unisons end the work in a spirit of some panache.

Brio and confidence account for much of the difference between this concerto and its predecessor. Three symphonies had emerged during the intervening years, as well as the three orchestral 'portraits of nature'. The concerto followed immediately on from *Symphony No 3* and takes the latter's concise working to further degrees of quiet virtuosity. Still, it is for the music's character as much as its deftness that it stands out, a venture into material that seems to pick up on European,and specifically 20th-century French, traditions of writing for wind instruments, so far an engaging one-off for him. The large number of performances has been justified by the response of audiences, which in turn, for once, is reflected in good reviews, reacting to the music's vitality and colour.

What could provoke a sequel to this? A piece written for a French flute player, perhaps?

PG: 'I put off the timpani concerto for about ten years because I just couldn't imagine how I would do it, and Jonathan Haas was so persistent that I finally did it. He was a complete nuisance until I wrote it.'

We have already met the *Concerto Fantasy For Two Timpanists And Orchestra* in passing, during the symphony chapter. In terms of performance it is not strictly the next concerto, by a couple of months, but its origins go back a long way – even before the saxophone quartet piece. Haas is the principal timpanist of the New York Chamber Orchestra, principal percussionist of the American Symphony Orchestra and a member of the American Composers Orchestra. He is also a relentless champion of his main instrument and has the distinction of performing the only solo timpani recital so far given at Carnegie Recital Hall, in 1980. Responsible for nearly 30 commissions of new timpani works, he had a pair of solo concertos in mind that he wanted from particular composers. One target was Frank Zappa, who died before Haas could get anywhere. With the other it was a different story. Like a good salesman, once he had Glass talking he never let him out of his sights and eventually he got his way, after a long series of postponements, other commissions intervening and, evidently, excuses. If you have read the symphony chapter, and seeing that Haas played for the American Composers Orchestra, you will probably have made a wrong guess about where the première took place. It was given on 19 November 2000 at Avery Fisher Hall in New York by another of Haas's orchestras, the American Symphony, with Haas and Svetoslav Stoyanov the soloists and the orchestra's music director Leon Botstein conducting. Several orchestras had been brought together to bring about the commission, with the American Symphony taking a leading role. Botstein offered to guarantee funding, although the project subsequently secured a 'Meet the Composer' grant. A large-scale tour followed in which

Haas was usually joined by the principal timpanist of each orchestra he visited. As yet there is no recording.

A timpani concerto is an improbable task for any composer to take on, and it turned even more improbable as it continued. One soloist became two. That was a contributed idea, and a helpful one, because if Haas wanted to play the piece with orchestras other than his own he would have to justify taking the place of the resident timpanists, who might well have wanted to wait until the solo rights were available for themselves (understandably enough: when else would they have a chance to solo with their own band?). Still, it had a knock-on effect on the logistics. During the composition, solo parts were passed back and forth between Glass, Haas and the percussionist Ian Finkel, who became involved in the editing and supplied one of the work's two alternative cadenzas; the other is by Glass. Glass made and recorded a four-hand piano reduction for use in rehearsals, which allowed further solo adjustments to be made across the duration of five sessions. Nine timpani divided between the soloists, mentioned in a preview notice by the American Symphony Orchestra, became 14.

The sight of a performance is therefore spectacular even before a note has been played, with this barrage of kettledrums set out at the front of the platform in the solo spot, rather than in the instruments' traditional place at the back or in a corner of the orchestra. Other percussion works have put various arrays of instruments before the public, but never before did so many timpani face them so directly. The only hint of a precursor is a short but famously exciting passage during the *Fourth Symphony* of the Danish composer Carl Nielsen, in which there is a fast and furious musical duel between two pairs of timpani playing in two different keys, on opposite sides of the orchestra – a passage audiences look forward to, and which always raises the temperature of the performance. There now appears to be a cult following for the *Concerto Fantasy*, which has specialist websites of its own beyond the usual unofficial Glass sites.

Once the music begins, the spectacle becomes a matter for the ear as much as the eye. Brash, noisy and irresistible, it is a diametrical opposite to the previous concerto with its teasing subtleties of colour. The subtleties are there – despite the final impression you will take away from a live experience, the scoring is full of light and shade and very carefully judged. It's just that, for a listener, the adrenalin rush takes over. The two soloists play almost continuously. This is a breathtakingly simple piece of unexpectedness. With solo instruments so thunderous and physically demanding, the obvious choice is to take regular breaks to rest arms and ears. So why be obvious? Why not go to the other extreme? The effect, especially in the dancing five- and seven-beat rhythms that are prominent in the quick music, is often like keeping up a groove. It's something that Western classical music never does with percussion. Only a handful of 20th-century works from Latin America, such as *Sensemaya* by Silvestre Revueltas, come near it. Other percussion concertos use a big range of instruments and rhythms to prevent the sense of a groove taking hold. Generally in orchestral music, percussion is used for emphasis, colour and peaks of excitement, and then it keeps quiet: the more sparing, the more effective, is the prevailing rule. Pop music on the other hand always keeps the percussion going. So does other people's art music. Indian hand drums are a familiar example, such as the tabla in North Indian music. But when it has two drummers going at it, the feel of the *Concerto Fantasy* is closer to African layered percussion, without in any sense sounding like an imitation or even being intentional. It just is what it is: daring and immediate.

The solo drum-strokes interlock, reinforce one another or add up. The relationship constantly shifts. Sometimes one or the other plays a melody in octaves with part of the orchestra. Sometimes there is an effect of playing in four-part chords, caused by the drums' resonance. Out of the collaborative work on the drum parts has grown an apparently endless variety of ways to use the instruments. When they play their cadenzas, between the second and last movements, they are joined by other orchestral percussion to explore material from the first (in Finkel's) or to juggle intricate patterns (in Glass's). They roll, they whisper, they thump, they sing. They are even required, just before the quick-fire end, to 'wail' in a chromatic combination of rolls and strokes. As for the bigger picture, the work is held together across the movements more by rhythmic than thematic links, and by the up-front orchestral colours, an unusually flamboyant sound in Glass's music from any period. The mood has its sombre episodes, especially in the subdued middle movement, but they are overwhelmed by energy, stemming from the physicality of the performance as well as the nature of the material. As it builds up its momentum it takes on a gleeful quality, a peculiar mix of wit and weight, that turns the finale into a massive, exhilarating fun piece with slightly ghoulish undertones. Afterwards it seems impossible for such apparently heavy resources to have moved with such pace and rhythmic vitality. But that is down to the tricks of the composing trade. It took several performances and further adjustments to the orchestration to bring about the necessary clarity. Listeners do not always realise how much fine tuning of this kind a new piece can need once it has been played – perhaps because many composers think they can get it right first time, or simply lose motivation once they move on to the next work. Nor do they expect that a composer as prolific as Glass, who frequently has four projects on the go at the same time, would worry away at the details after the event and keep on going back to them. But he discusses such experiences below, in the context of the *Cello Concerto*.

The two remaining concertos performed up until mid-2002, also still unrecorded for commercial release, have certain features in common. They feature unarguably mainstream solo instruments, and they are similarly focused in their form, drawing on what is now a substantial amount of symphonic experience and still having distinctive features of their own. Both are dominated by long, positively luxuriant slow movements, which generate an unprecedented quantity of frank, extended, warmly lyrical melody. Both have compact, dance-like finales, which head with increasing animation towards their definitive statements, or rather states of being, and promptly stop. The first of them is for piano and strings. It was premièred a little earlier than the *Concerto Fantasy*, on 22 September 2000. Dennis Russell Davies had wanted Glass to write a concerto in which he could play the solo part himself as well as conducting. The commission was brought about by the annual contemporary music festival in Austria that first presented it, Festival Klangspuren, partnered by Tirol-Werbung – an infrastructure organization responsible for promoting tourism – and the Stuttgart Chamber

Orchestra, which gave the première. When it emerged, it bore the title *Tirol Concerto*. It opens with the piano alone, and a theme that sounds strangely like a chorale and completely unlike Glass, except for it being harmonized in a rather personal way with a leaning towards ambiguous chords using flattened degrees of the scale:

PG: 'That's the Tirol! I was commissioned by the Tirol board of tourist development and they had the idea that if people knew something about Tirolean culture, more of them would go to Tirol. This is a part of Austria in the mountains where there's a lot of skiing. They said, would I write a *Tirol Concerto* and I said, what would that be, and they said we'll send you some music volumes with the theme and could it appear in the concerto? That was the commission. I said, send me the music and let me look at it. So what you hear at the beginning is a Tirolean folk song which of course sounds like folk songs from all over the world, in the way that folk songs have that quality of always being familiar. I reharmonized it, but it's their melody. I actually dropped out one phrase which was redundant, I trimmed it a little bit. But if you play this in Austria everyone recognizes it, and I thought it was kind of fun to do.'

RM: 'Then the big tune in the middle movement relates to it, and one of the themes in the last movement relates back to that.'

PG: 'It does, it does. If you listen to the whole concerto it does seem like a whole piece, doesn't it? It's been a successful piece. Dennis [Russell Davies] is performing it, right now it's his piece. Just strings and piano, a very nice combination, and it's a piece that can be done by a lot of community orchestras and smaller groups, if you have a good piano player. A lot of places in this country [the US] have chamber orchestras or full orchestras, but to use a string section makes it a little easier for them. Like the *Violin Concerto* I really set out to write a popular piece. I did it for a lot of reasons, besides which Dennis is a good piano player. I thought I would play it myself. As I was writing it I realised it had reached the point where it was already beyond my capabilities. I could learn to play it. I reckon it would take me three months of work and I'm not inclined to do that. I have better things to do than learn to play a piano concerto.'

In aspiring to popularity he seems to have hit the button again. As with the *Symphony No 6* the word has yet to get around and the real test of that aspiration is still in the future. But the piece is in demand, always performed by Davies so far, and it is being well received. Extracts have been used in an 11-minute film, *Impressions Of Tirol*, by Georg Rina. Once the concerto gets onto record, which it will do after the US première in March 2003 when Davies and the Stuttgart Orchestra are booked to visit New York for a concert at the Metropolitan Museum, you can be confident that it will do the rounds fully. Radio stations will go for it and other pianists will want it. The reason for confidence, from a listener's point of view, is clear: it is the slow movement. It dominates the concerto in its duration – 17 minutes out of the work's 28 in total – and in its positively high-romantic atmosphere. The feeling of intense calm is similar to that of the corresponding movement in Beethoven's *Emperor Concerto*, and so is one aspect of its form, at least for the first few minutes: a long, slow, solemn melody on strings, a piano entry immediately afterwards, a little later the harmonies of the theme beneath arpeggios. That is as far as passing similarities go because the movement is really a set of variations on the opening melody. The melody itself, however, is the big thing about the music. It is beautifully shaped out of three phrases, which repeat in the pattern AABCBC. The A and B phrases are eloquent enough, but the rocking figure of C gives the melody an unexpected final extension, enough to turn it from shapely to memorably inspired.

If Glass's father might have liked the *Violin Concerto*, all the customers in his record shop who bought up the favourite romantic piano concertos (and presumably stopped him taking them home to check out) would be clamouring for this. It is just the start of a sustained and searching exploration of the material, and of a mood that is unfamiliar in Glass's music up to this point. The variation form is related to the repeating blocks of music that feature in earlier slow movements such as the *Violin Concerto* and the *Symphony No 3*. But since the melody plays for a minute and a half it has a completely different effect, and indeed it takes a different course, not piling up additional layers but rearranging the elements. In any case you are three minutes into the music before you realise it might be shaping up as variations because the first variation, with the piano playing the melody and then handing the lead back to the strings to extend while it starts ornamenting, sounds more like a restatement. After that the harmonies of the theme begin to recur while new ideas are floated out over them. During the final stages the violins extend the last phrase of the melody over and over, eventually recalling the first variation while the piano has a last bite at the theme.

It is difficult to overstate the impact of this movement because, in one leap, it gets past the whole 'new romantic' area that has been exploited by many American composers contemporary with Glass, usually holding on to elements of contemporary procedures that add a touch of post-modern sophistication and academic respectability. This is full-blown romantic expression with no irony and no apologies. The Austrian connection, in the sense of the country's pre-modernist musical history, seems to have insinuated its way into the very heart of the work. In comparison the rest of the concerto feels subordinate to it, like a prelude and epilogue, although the whole work is ingeniously organized and fetching. It certainly gets off to a friendly start with the Tirolean tune. Perhaps the obvious thing to do, having decided to work with a donated theme, would be to write variations on it. The *Tirol Concerto* is more subtle. Once played, the tune never reappears. It seems to have been thrown away as spectacularly as Tchaikovsky did with the famous opening tune in his first piano concerto, but Glass has been sly. Instead the tune is constantly there, in disguise. The variations Glass does write are on a variation of the tune, in that the slow movement's melody starts out from a fresh look at the melodic outline of its first two phrases. Then the finale's dance theme, in turn, makes parts of this melody evolve one step further.

So the disappearance of the Tirol is temporary. While it is out of earshot, the rest of the first movement, running for just another five minutes, takes off into a livelier but quite easy-going kaleidoscope of ideas. Rippling oscillations between major and minor make up the main recurrent feature, punctuated by a characteristic mix of extensions and new elements, notably a strong descending phrase towards the end, which leads towards a wind-down and an expectant pause – the moment when the strings launch their great melody. Right through, the piano takes the lead and it does so with a consistently richer texture than Glass's usual rather spare writing for the instrument. The substantial chords are like a translation of his often fat-toned brass scoring, but mixed with arpeggios and scales they have in this context a curious resemblance to Schubert – at least, they do as played by Davies, who has 19th-century Austrian music in his bones. In the equally compact finale the quietly good-humoured ambience returns at a pace, and the dance character takes on an escalating sense of joy until descending phrases once again come to dominate and end the music promptly.

The *Cello Concerto* was commissioned by the Beijing Music Festival for the 50th birthday of its soloist, Julian Lloyd Webber, and premièred by the China Philharmonic, conducted by Long Yu on 21 October 2001. Glass had not been looking to write for solo cello, and once again the idea came from the performer. When Lloyd Webber asked him for a concerto, Glass gave the usual response – sort yourself out a commission. Beijing was where it came up. So far, however, it has had only one other performance, in New Zealand during April 2002. There is a reason, and it is down to the stage of the concerto's life at which this book finds it:

PG: 'You get a lot of performances of concertos, like the violin concerto, which has been recorded several times. Now I've a piano concerto which is starting to go through something similar. There's the saxophone quartet concerto which has been played about 80 times. It becomes very effective in the soloist's career to have a piece like that. We're just getting the cello concerto together, we have to do a little rewriting in the third movement because you can't hear it that well.'

RM: 'I was going to ask you what was happening in the last minute. Is he playing? In the tape of the première it sounds like what happens at the end of *Harold In Italy* by Berlioz, where the viola soloist gets carried away in a kind of big dance and just emerges at the very end.'

PG: 'That's nice if that were true, there's a certain amount of that but I have to rescore it. That often happens with concertos. The timpani concerto has been done a lot of times. With that one, the orchestration wasn't resolved until the fifth performance. Concertos can be very tricky that way.'

RM: 'The timpani concerto has the soloists playing almost continuously from start to finish, they're always doing something, they're accompanying, they're playing melodies or duets and they are really soloists.'

PG: 'And you can hear it. You can hear the orchestra too. That one worked out very well eventually, the violin concerto worked well, the piano concerto worked very well. None of those were in the final form when I worked on them, they all had to be rewritten. You can't go by recordings because we've gotten used to hearing a different balance in the studio. You can fix them up. But concertos, they really get played, so they have to work.

'Sometimes a conductor will help a lot with orchestration: Dennis Davies helped a lot with the violin concerto. It really comes down to dynamics and doublings and what octaves people are playing in, something very specific. What's easier when you write these things is to over-write a little bit and then cut them back. That always happens because I write down what instruments I think could be playing, but then it always gets cut back a little. You should be hearing the cello all the way through, and when you're not hearing him then he doesn't need to play at all. He plays an awful lot so he needs to take some breaks.'

RM: 'It does seem to have a terrific focus and clarity overall though, for instance, the lyrical line that goes through the middle movement.'

PG: 'I like this piece very much, I think the concerto works in the second movement, you can hear it pretty well. The problem is in the third movement. I know how to do it, it's just finding the time to do it. There have been two performances so far but I think we'll wait until I redo the third movement.'

When that is done, like the *Tirol Concerto* it is going to be picked up. The reason is the same, an astonishing slow movement that even by the standards of Glass's recent music takes off lyrically with an intense radiance. It does not dominate the rest of the concerto to the same extreme extent, but at 15 minutes long, running for around half the concerto's duration, it creates a powerful presence at the heart of the work. The other movements this time, however, are more substantial in their own right. While the opening movement is predominantly moderate in pace and also lyrical, the cello sets a purposeful tone at the outset. Repeating broken-chord phrases, modal in flavour, expand and shift their harmonies over spare, dark-hued orchestral support. The solo line grows like a cadenza as the figuration intensifies, then returns to first thoughts. A short surge forwards, led by the orchestra, subsides into an extensive cello melody, which spreads itself through the centre of the movement, initially in dialogue with woodwind and later over a drone. In the final two minutes the music reanimates itself with high glockenspiel and woodwind playing broken chords above the cello, and slows again to its conclusion.

Pulsing, syncopated chords, rich in horn tone, set the slow movement going. The top line of the chords is dominated by alternations between neighbouring notes of the scale, giving the music a distinctive melodic shape, which is soon picked up and extended by the cello. A new descending phrase echoes the lyrical material of the first movement; orchestral violins soar and trill and make a dialogue with the cello. From midway, the earlier phrases drift back and take over the foreground. Oscillations and scales spread out through the orchestra, the violins soar again and again then the cello resumes its melodic meditation and leads through to a spacious conclusion on a minor chord.

If this is the music's core, the finale is its surprise, even in the provisional version so far played. The cello begins as it did the whole work, varying the line slightly with a held note at the end of each phrase. Then the music suddenly catches fire. A long, clashing crescendo, essentially built on one complex chord, takes it up to a state of brassy, shrill agitation. Briefly the cello turns lyrical, then solo brass take over the line until the cello establishes a dancing pulse. Slower chordal outbursts intervene, but the manic dance character begins to sweep away all before it. As it continues in the orchestra, the cello, in a high register, reviews its earlier ideas until it is swept up in the tumult that, in turn, dances its way back to the first orchestral outburst, which is by now suggesting a desperate exuberance bordering on ecstasy. High, descending figures on the cello and four low-pitched unisons bring the piece to an abrupt end. This is the main passage that Glass wants to revise, so that the cello's role is clarified: it remains highly active and needs to be heard. Already, however, the music possesses an exciting, edgy and almost dangerous character, which gives the preceding luxuriance a more far-reaching expressive and symphonic context.

Glass's concert music also includes solo piano and organ music, string quartets and, for orchestra, the three 'portraits of nature' that began with *The Light*. In their various ways they have all developed their musical media and several of them are secure in the contemporary repertoire. From the perspective of what Glass is doing now, however, the symphonic and concerto developments show much more of immediate interest – hence their focus in these two chapters. The most recent of them (the *Cello Concerto*, the *Tirol Concerto* and the *Symphony No 6*) are still relatively little known. They are unheard in many musical centres, none of them is yet available on a commercial recording and very few people have listened to all three of them. This survey is therefore something of a report back from the future. But it is going to stick its neck out. These three are major pieces that between them should rewrite the reputation of Glass as a symphonic composer. They show a new expressive frankness within his instrumental work and a confident virtuosity in his personal style of handling large-scale abstract forms.

As the background of these pieces has shown, Glass never set out to compose a substantial line of concert works, and on one level to make too much of it is to distort his central preoccupation with music as part of a larger dramatic experience. Yet it cannot be a distortion, because he chose to take on the commissions and he let his creative energies do what they could with the projects. The body of works has become too big to sideline. The more the symphonic work and the instrumental work grows, and the more it is disseminated on recordings, the more these works are going to be the way most people get to know about Glass compared with the number of people who are able to experience the operas. There is another point: the symphonic works and the operas are growing closer together. Glass's use of the orchestra started in the opera house, and so did his handling of larger forms. The last two symphonies have used voices and moved into dramatic handling of texts. Concertos are inherently dramatic, but Glass's have moved from the still relatively reflective *Violin Concerto* to an altogether more highly charged scenario in the *Cello Concerto*. It is often said of Mozart that his piano concertos and his operas were two sides of the same coin, which dealt in the currency of dramatic expression and human truth. There is no copyright on that attitude to artistic endeavour, and it would increasingly seem that Glass too has found his own way towards it.

Next in line from Glass was a harpsichord concerto, due to have been completed and performed during the second half of 2002 while this book was in the press. That may be something else again, but readers will have to find out for themselves.

Scene 5
Explorers On Stage And Screen

Glass may have become an opera composer by accident, but he is staying one on his own terms. His subjects are his own choice, and he seeks out the circumstances for making the stage works possible. It is the opposite of the situation with his orchestral works, which have been fruitful responses to unsought requests. While he is best known for his theatre music, the works themselves (apart from the first three, *Einstein On The Beach, Satyagraha* and *Akhnaten*) are not his best known. They have had widely varying fortunes after their première runs. Some of them are revived or given new stagings, while others of them seem to have been displaced from opera houses' attention by the constant arrival of new works somewhere else. All of them receive international attention to the extent that there is media interest in the premières but few of them have received consistent international exposure to audiences.

These are unique circumstances for a successful opera composer in the present day. Less prolific composers' stage works are all well known in at least one or two places. Their fame may not spread far beyond their own country, or in the United States their own part of the country, but there it is at least based on widespread experience of their output. It is remarkable that *Satyagraha* and *Akhnaten* have been seen in so many productions and places through two decades. For almost any composer, that kind of exposure for two full-length works would be enough to know them by. We are, however, not talking about almost any composer but the one who has kept on surprising the opera public with fresh twists and departures for a quarter of a century. It is unreasonable to expect the same theatres to present a new Glass production every year: they would doubtless all find an audience, but there are local composers and other repertoire to consider. This leaves an element of frustration for followers of Glass, which has no easy solution, at least in terms of live performance. Fairly soon it will be possible to see recordings and relays of nearly everything through the spread of electronic media, and that will be the time when the sheer quantity of Glass's theatrical output makes its full impact.

That will also be the time for a survey of the stage work that attempts the same level of detail as the preceding two chapters. Writers and audiences alike will be in a position to draw on a full experience. Until then, nobody has that experience. This book reported an opinion of *Galileo Galilei* at second hand because the first performances of Glass's most recent opera have a certain news value around the time of publication. That is an exception: the rest of the book is based on direct knowledge of the music. If it has not been possible to get to know a work, it is not given detailed coverage, along with areas of the music – mostly early – that have had too much written about them already. Opera and film music both fall into one category or the other. This is why they do not loom as large in the book as they have actually done in Glass's life.

Nevertheless, if this book needs to get one big message across about the opera and theatre work, it is precisely that continuing central role it has in his life. The message is particularly necessary in a context that has insisted, against current opinion and awareness, that Glass's concert music is now of some consequence. Theatre still rules, even when we do not get to see the operas often enough.

From a musical angle some of the theatre work has featured in the first chapter. There are still some points to make on the dramatic themes, which give many of the individual works taken together a kind of unity in diversity. If there is a ruling idea that runs from beginning to end, it is the urge of the human spirit to widen its horizons and to drive itself into the unknown. Exploration, whether geographical, scientific or social; the pursuit of an obsession; the power of art and religion; the will to change the world with ideas – all these broadly related themes persist through the whole body of work. The body now numbers about 20, depending on where you draw the provisional line that separates theatre pieces from music with a theatrical dimension, and what you call a one-off oddball such as *Hydrogen Jukebox* in which the words of Allen Ginsberg are selected and arranged to present a 'portrait of America' over four decades using singers and (when he was alive) Ginsberg's own narration. As of 2002, Glass's first and last major theatre pieces are about the nature of great scientists concerned with particular aspects of experience. Both Einstein and Galileo pursued mould-breaking investigations of movement and light: the effect of movement in relation to the speed of light in the former case, the evidence of planetary movement revealed by a telescope in the latter. Another experiment on the speed of light comes up outside the theatre as the motivation for Glass's orchestral piece *The Light*, while in writing film music for *A Brief History Of Time* he homed in on Stephen Hawking's famous exposition of the theories that bound these discoveries together.

Two epic-scale works move their preoccupations out to exploration and discovery on a global front. *The Voyage* was Glass's commission for the Metropolitan Opera in New York, at the venue where *Einstein On The Beach* had first amazed the American public 16 years before as a visiting performance on the company's day off. The year was 1992 and the occasion was the 500th anniversary of Christopher Columbus's journey to America, or 'discovery of America' as it is still often called as though nobody knew it was there until somebody showed up from Europe. Nothing quite so naïve here: Glass wrote the basic story for the work and the cosmopolitan playwright David Henry Hwang made a libretto from it. The tone is allegorical, touching on the nature of the exploratory spirit and the inevitable phenomenon of clashing cultures that follows as soon as people turn up in a place they do not know, and centring on the question of what they are looking for when they are driven to travel.

'Christopher Columbus', Glass has written, 'stands for all those eternal travellers – Ulysses, Noah, Flying Dutchman – doomed or destined, alone with his idea on a boat; he is a stand-in for all voyagers, for all those compelled to explore, to question.' And even for Einstein or Gandhi, Roderick Usher or Orpheus or the Beast who pursued Beauty. This is the central preoccupation at its most direct. It had had a previous airing in a big, five-act, barely known work devised the year before in collaboration with Robert Wilson, and not performed until 1998 in Lisbon where it had been commissioned. *White Raven* took off from the explorations of another Latin adventurer, Vasco da Gama, and also concerned itself with meanings beyond the literal: as Glass put it, 'an open reflection on the concept of discovery of commencement (of what does not exist but comes into being) and the concept of beginning'.

Gandhi was at the centre of *Satyagraha*, Glass's second major stage work and his first to be written for an opera company. The period of Gandhi's life it covers was not the triumphant movement that ousted the British from control of India, but his early years as a lawyer in South Africa when he reacted to the colonial powers' exclusion of Indians, like Africans, from political and social life by devising most of the strategies and techniques of non-violent action that he put into practice throughout his life. Told that he had staged an idealized image of Gandhi, Glass said that he was indeed trying to present the image, the Gandhi of universal human perceptions, rather than a biographical study. The sense of mythologizing history is reinforced by the presence looking down on the action, one in each act of the opera, of three non-singing images of figures who personify related aspects of history and creative discovery: Tagore, Tolstoy and Martin Luther King.

Another world-changer, the Pharaoh Akhnaten, was the subject of Glass's next opera. This time the wider concern was religious thought as a vehicle for human development, specifically the substitution of monotheism for the worship of many gods – a policy that had tragic consequences for its instigator, who was violently removed from power by the religious opposition, but beyond its local circumstances foreshadowed the momentous impact of the single-god religions that came to dominate much of the world in the following millennium.

There are three works that pick up on central themes of the author and film-maker Jean Cocteau, concerned with the power of imagination and the clash between misunderstood, creative individuals and their social environment. The first was a version of Cocteau's take on the myth of Orpheus; the third, a 'dance-opera spectacle' with singers and dancers taking turns, was *Les Enfants Terribles*. Most ingenious and ambitious of them is the second, *La Belle Et La Bête*, an opera which was conceived and originally performed as a replacement for the soundtrack of Cocteau's film: the singing parts are synchronized with the speech of the actors.

Another planned trilogy uses science fiction as a means of exploring human survival and evolution, taking novels from the *Canopus In Argos* series by Doris Lessing. This collaboration with Lessing as librettist began in the mid-1980s and has moved more slowly – only two operas so far exist. The first of them is one of Glass's 'vanished' major works. The *Making Of The Representative For Planet Eight* was co-commissioned by houses in Houston, London and Kiel and given high-profiled premières starting in July 1988. Then it disappeared from view: 'We did *The Marriages Between Zones Three, Four And Five*, in Heidelberg and Chicago,' Glass said earlier this year, referring to the second Lessing opera – itself not seen until 1997 – 'but I kind of liked *Planet Eight*. It was very well received at the time but I don't know what happened to it. I've written so many operas since then and it's not an opera people have wanted to do.' Memories of the London première are of a strong impact undermined by a sense, in the later stages, that the text was running out of time for the music. Large sections of it ended up spoken. Had everything been set the performance might have run for several hours. 'We meant to revise it and we've said that we would do it. Doris has agreed to revisions and cuts in the text, but there's no point in doing it if we don't have the producer. Not everything happens.'

A piece much less likely to happen again is *Monsters Of Grace*, another theatre collaboration between Glass and Robert Wilson and possibly the final one. It was a characteristic reach out into the technical unknown that involved film, stage and the poetry of Jalal-ud-din Rumi, first put on in provisional form at UCLA, Los Angeles in 1998 and later taken on tour, still with sections of film missing. The preparation had been fraught with difficulties that left a bad taste. There was a clash with Wilson over rehearsal procedure that left Glass out of sorts, and this has had a knock-on effect: the two men had been talking for years about a project called *Arabian Nights* – intended as a companion piece to *White Raven* – and this work, so potentially appropriate to an America newly ill at ease with the Arabic world, has evidently gone into limbo. The main problem with *Monsters Of Grace* itself turned out to be financial. 'The producer ran out of money and never finished the film. Bob was unhappy with it, it was not realized the way it was meant to be. The producer was inexperienced at film-making. There were things like colour correction that he hadn't allowed for. When it got to the point when it was time to do revisions, he hadn't budgeted that time. It wasn't intentional but it certainly compromised our ability to finish the work. When it went to London, four of the scenes had to be done as stage pieces. It was presented as a hybrid and it wasn't so bad, people liked it, but it wasn't what we meant to do. In a certain way it was a disaster, so much money and so unfinished. I don't think you'll ever see it now.'

Other works have had better fortunes, among them *Les Enfants Terribles* and the 1988 version of *The Fall Of The House Of Usher* by another of Baltimore's creative sons, Edgar Allan Poe, both of which have current productions. What you may have a chance to see for yourself remains something of a global lottery. Whatever it is, however, it will be part of a wider theatrical perspective that has occupied Glass since the 1960s and can also be experienced in some of his films, despite the different motivations that have brought about his collaborations with film-makers and his scores for existing scenarios.

Many times, Glass has expressed a sceptical point of view about films and the industry that makes them:

PG: 'I wouldn't say that the film industry is interested in the enterprise of good films at all. Basically it's an entertainment industry, interested in making money by entertaining people. That's all it is. In that environment there are people making very good movies. I think *Kundun* was a very good movie, I think *Mishima* was. *Koyaanisqatsi* is not an industry film, *Powaqqatsi* is not an industry film. There are lots of independent film-makers who do work of quality, but the industry itself does not encourage work of quality – it's an entertainment system. It's important when we work in film that we understand the parameters and the limits and the possibilities. If you're working on a commercial movie then the artistic choices will be more limited. If you're working on an independent movie, it may have higher aspirations. For instance they don't have the money to fire you. Once they've hired you they are kind of stuck with you, whereas the industry films can go through two or three composers before they end up with a score that they like. Still, everyone will be paid.'

RM: 'Do you actively seek film work, apart from the art movies?'

PG: 'We do have good connections with people in Hollywood, but the thing is, if somebody's making a commercial movie they normally ask Hans Zimmer or James Horner – they are not stupid, they get commercial film composers. When I get to do a film it's usually an art film of some kind. It's a little bit offbeat. Fortunately I play in LA every year, I play at Royce Hall where the UCLA is and I do live music projects with film all the time there and I meet many film composers at those events, so I'm quite well known for the music that I do.

'Some results I like, some I don't like. With film I have very little control over the whole thing. The medium is controlled by, not even the director but more the producer, and the studio and the accountants. Only the independent movies are controlled by the directors. It's not a medium which is composer-friendly at all, even though it's clear that the contribution of composers is fundamental to the work.'

The good news for admirers of the two non-industry classics *Koyaanisqatsi* and *Powaqqatsi* is that the third member of the trilogy, planned since the 1980s, has been made. Funding to complete it finally came together in 2001. All three, directed by Godfrey Reggio, are concerned with the ambivalent impact of technology and Western values on life around the world. In *Koyaanisqatsi* the imagery contrasted the frantic life of cities and motorways with the stillness of natural scenes and the evolution of skyscapes. Its speeded up sequences of traffic and pedestrians, and clouds growing and shrinking, have passed into the common consciousness. This happened not so much because many people saw the film, rather as the result of its influence on other film-makers and particularly on the directors of music videos and advertisements. It is hard to go through an evening's television anywhere in the world without manically whizzing road systems or self-building mountains of cumulus showing up during at least one commercial break.

Powaqqatsi went on to show the steady encroachment of Westernized behaviour, consumer mentality and high technology on traditional ways of life around the world – a study of globalization before anybody used the word. It did not pass judgment and left viewers to form their own conclusions about the benefits of advances in living standards and the loss of old ways. Unlike *Koyaanisqatsi*, which drew from Glass one of his best-known syntheses of sustained gloom and high-speed musical action, *Powaqqatsi* has a much more relaxed and often joyous score that is notable for being one of the few in which Glass directly incorporates elements of music from other cultures.

Now there is *Naqoyqatsi*. This is about human self-destruction and specifically war:

PG: 'We were making the film at that period in September when everyone was freaking out, and there have been enough wars around to make the piece very current. It's not liable to go out of fashion. War is big business these days; there's a lot of interest in war [sardonic laugh]. The film is made with digital technology, and the images are about 80 per cent digital. About 20 per cent are film. It's very much made from images that have been affected by high-technology ways of filming, for instance using cameras that do 500 frames a second. Unbelievably detailed images. And then these images are processed through other kinds of technology so that the whole film is – well, you can't really film a film like this, you have to fabricate it. It's the dance Godfrey's been having with technology that began with *Koyaanisqatsi*, and this may well be the ultimate form of it.

'As for the relationship with the music, we've pretty much turned it around. At this point the music is based on treatments of ideas, and he did most of the cutting and fabrication of images to the music. I didn't see so much footage, and it was in such a primitive state when I saw it that I can't really say that the score was based very much on that. There was an ongoing discussion that began about that time, so we had talked about it for a decade. Then we divided the film into sections, into movements, and it became fairly easy to work on. Sometimes I didn't know what the images were. Often I wrote music and he did the images. There were interludes that were created after the whole film was done, and he found images for them.'

RM: 'Is there a different sound to the music compared to the others – more than the difference from *Koyaaniqaatsi* to *Powaqqatsi*?'

PG: 'It's quite different again. This is more of a symphonic piece, and there's a soloist who plays all of the way through. The cello – it's Yo Yo Ma – becomes almost the voice of the piece. The sound of the piece is very much affected by the fact that there's a solo instrument that weaves through it. It's not totally that way, but in the same way that *Powaqqatsi* is distinguished by the world music sources that I used, and *Koyaanisqatsi* is conditioned by the ensemble – it sounds like it's built from my ensemble – this feels like a big symphonic picture for the soloist, it really affects how the piece is heard.'

Glass's latest 'a little bit offbeat' commission from the American industry was *The Hours*, a film due for release at the end of December 2002. The film is based on a 1998 Pulitzer Prize-winning novel by Michael Cunningham, which is in turn a homage to *Mrs Dalloway* by the British author Virginia Woolf. The UK interest continues in that David Hare wrote the screenplay and Stephen Daldry directs. As arty as Hollywood gets, it is an intimate character study that interweaves the stories of three women at three different times in the last 80 years, the earliest being about Virginia Woolf herself. They are played by Nicole Kidman (as Woolf), Julianne Moore and Meryl Streep.

Opportunities such as this come the way of classical composers only rarely, and Glass is aware of the value of putting his music before a vast public that would probably not otherwise have come into contact with it:

PG: 'A film like *Kundun* has been seen by millions of people. There we're getting into a real mainstream audience, far more than concerts or opera: films like *Kundun* or *Koyaanisqatsi* or most of all *The Truman Show*. In that one only half the music is mine and of the half, I'd say that 80 per cent was written before, so only ten per cent is new. But it doesn't matter because the point is that most of the people that go to see *The Truman Show* never went to a concert, never went to an opera anyway. It's all new to them, they've never heard it before. I'm just finishing another film which promises to be a rather commercial movie because it has actual movie stars in it. I've seen *The Hours*, I've done the score already and it's a very beautiful movie. That will be seen by probably more people than saw *Truman*; it's hard to tell, you don't know how these things will go. People buy film music because it reminds them of the movie, their motivations are a bit different. They will be buying it not because my name is attached to it but because people are attached to it who are not on the record. Nicole Kidman is quite capable of singing, she's not singing on the record. Maybe it would be better if she was, but it didn't work out that way!'

Even these industry movies engage to some extent with Glass's perennial dramatic fascinations: Virginia Woolf is the archetypal artist out of joint with her milieu, while the central character of *The Truman Show* is another man 'alone with his idea on a boat', literally so at the end when he sets off to test his suspicion that the world is not what he thought. This is the film that in 1997 anticipated European television's *Big Brother* series by imagining that one man is on screen live for 24 hours a day being his natural self – the twist being that he is the only person in the world not to know the whole of his life has taken place in a studio and everybody he meets is played by an actor.

Of other films that reflect his interests, *Mishima* was made in 1985 by Paul Schrader about the Japanese writer Yukio Mishima. This single-minded, and in the end spectacularly suicidal, figure espoused a portfolio of unsavoury and narcissistic activities ranging from right-wing politics to body building. Life and art as connected incompatibles: the structure of the film interwove dramatized sections drawn from his novels with biographical episodes, enclosed by the day of his death. Glass put these three elements of the film to music for three different groups, respectively a full orchestra, a string quartet and a string orchestra. The 'biographical' music found a second life as a concert suite, which Glass has said was his intention all along: this is his *String Quartet No 3*, the six movements of which have graphic titles such as 'Grandmother And Kimitake' and indeed 'Body Building'.

Most involving for general and musical audiences alike, perhaps, is *Kundun*. Martin Scorsese's 1997 film is a dramatization of the early years of the Dalai Lama, which culminates in the Tibetan leader's escape from his Chinese-occupied homeland across the Himalayan mountains. It was a labour of love for the director, who is a prominent supporter of the ongoing exiled government based in India and himself a Tibetan Buddhist. Cast entirely from ordinary Tibetan people living outside the country, it contained no star names and was modestly successful as a commercial release. It remains one of Scorsese's most admired films. One of the reasons for this was its unusually unified treatment of the score that his fellow Buddhist and like-minded collaborator had composed. It really was a collaboration, at least up to a point, not as even-handed as the Godfrey Reggio artistic relationship but in its final stages presenting a musical sequence lasting through ten minutes of mountain panoramas, which were cut to the music rather than vice versa.

Glass responded to this relative openness with a score of symphonic scope for full orchestra – or what sounds like a full orchestra: see the next chapter for some insight into the recording techniques that are used in Glass's studio where the soundtrack was made. Tibetan horns and chanting monks, the sounds familiar to all who visit Dharamsala, Sikkkim or Ladakh, appear in the soundtrack too, integrated into the score but not influencing the musical language, which remains as personal as ever. The result is a near-perfect balance between speech, music and camerawork and, for many, a haunting introduction to a spiritual tradition and to a musical world, both of which stay long in the memory.

Scene 6
A Working Life

PG: 'As you see, in this place there are two recording studios, there's my publishing company, the booking company is up in the front and the lawyer who does a lot of the legal work rents office space. This is a publishing company, it's a production company and a record company. It's become a workplace which has allowed me to be extremely productive.

'I'm about to start a harpsichord concerto; I should have started it yesterday [this was early May 2002], I've been finishing up some other things right now. The film score for *The Hours* I'm finishing, and the rewrites for *Galileo* have already begun – fitting music to singers' voices. The concerto should be done by the end of June. It's to be played in September so I'm bound to finish it. After that I have two one-act operas for ART, a small theatre company in Boston. So it's important for me to do that, it keeps that part of my work alive. I have tours in the fall. That could keep me busy until November.'

After minimalist, the favourite lazy person's adjective for Glass is workaholic. One is about as true as the other. If you choose to follow the direction of this book by listening to the works it discusses, you will run into the elements of minimalism early on. Its existence at that time is a fact. Then the elements become the elements of a personal musical language. The language takes on many more elements, and the minimalist days are soon left behind. To think otherwise is to ignore all the music's dimensions except for a handful of familiar elements. Likewise, it is a fact that Glass works a lot. He takes on projects when he is already busy, he accepts commissions that apparently distract him from his main artistic focus and, as preceding chapters have shown, he has composed a substantial body of orchestral music without ever intending to. The adjective is not exactly discouraged by the results. Workaholic, however, speaks not about results but about the process of getting them and the attitude to getting them, and in that context the word has overtones of joylessness, which are not appropriate. It says instead something about the person who uses the word: maybe they do not like the music and are depressed by how much there is, maybe they are themselves a slow worker or maybe they just hate their own work.

Prolific composers in recent times have often attracted negative criticism. People who are quite at ease with the productivity of Mozart or Schubert, which is safely in the past and a known, fixed quantity, are unsettled by the amount that composers within living memory such as Milhaud or Martinu could write, and unsettled even more if the composer is currently active. Critics who could not have known more than a fraction of Milhaud's output will routinely dismiss it as patchy, uneven or handicapped by its sheer size: a convenient opinion that makes it unnecessary to bother with seeking out the rest, and more a symptom of personal dislike than a critical judgment. If you do not think much of Glass's music, how comforting it must be to know that there is so much out there you could be rude about and so much more still to come, if it were ever necessary to go to the trouble of listening to it. Instead of experiencing the impact of *Symphony No 6* you can simply point to the existence of a dozen other pieces written within a year or two as a reason for keeping it at arm's length.

There is an appropriate adjective for Glass's working practice: focused. No creative person works in a joyless way. Creating is too essential a part of the human being. The work itself takes over. It is too demanding to be done in a reluctant way; the effect would be soul-destroying and the person would give up, as some artists do when their energies have run out, either temporarily or permanently. The compulsion to compose is irresistible but it is not work for work's sake; it is a consequence of what you are, not just something you do, and attitudes to it are beside the point. However, you can make it easy for yourself and you can make it difficult; you can arrange your working life with intelligence and efficiency or you can let it get out of control. It is in this area that Glass clearly has an additional skill beyond the creative ones. What this skill amounts to is arranging life so that creative time is maximized while other functions are kept at a distance (but are still under his control). Then the musical training and the mindset come into play, and the focus can be as sharp as possible.

This is a disciplined approach and it has several sources: family history, temperament, Nadia Boulanger's demands as a teacher and her personal example and the practice of Tibetan Buddhism, which he had begun to study in the early 1960s, a little before he went to Paris. There is more about the Paris days in the next chapter, and the parallels between his musical training and Buddhist practice are the subject of a published interview, which he gave in 1992 to the American magazine *Tricycle*. 'Boulanger carried the idea of discipline to another level,' he said there. 'She added something that I became familiar with later through Tibetan practice, something that I can only describe as a devotional aspect of music study. Boulanger set herself up as an incomparable model of discipline and dedication… Yet, she did it in a very simple way.'

There is also what non-Americans would see as a very American, self-sufficient way of planning and managing a working life. Glass's father started out in Baltimore repairing cars, moved onto radios, sold records through his radio business, developed a record shop, added a branch outlet that his two sons ran for a while and turned into a kind of musical guru for the local record-buying public – all part of the personal service. Glass himself studied music in Baltimore from age eight, the youngest-ever student at the city's Peabody Institute, and moved on at 15 to the University of Chicago as a mathematics and philosophy undergraduate. He operated a crane for six months to finance further studies at the Juilliard School of Music in New York. In his early days as a barely earning professional musician he worked as a plumber. At the time of *Einstein On The Beach* he drove a cab. The day after the première he was told by a passenger who saw his name that he shared the name with 'a very famous composer'. Published cartoons that now hang on the wall of his New York office base refer to anecdotes about those days. In one of them he was working at the home of the Australian-born art critic Robert Hughes, who recognized him and was shocked that an artist should be installing his dishwasher.

Glass has said he was 41 before he could support himself from his music alone, and his hard-working habits have not only died hard but have put him at an advantage. They have freed him from the need to support his composing with a salaried position, like the professorships that many composers hold, or to become dependent on public funding as his European contemporaries often are. They have given him the ability to keep his management and publishing himself, rather than assigning them to agents and outside companies in return for a percentage or a share of the rights. He himself is able to do the commercial work that keeps the enterprise going and allows him to spend as much time as possible on the projects that are closest to his heart. His company set-up is organized as an efficient way to deal with the income generated and to exploit the rights in the music. It suits him to work in an unusual mix of media and to use a very wide range of outlets, even if it surprises composers who do not like getting their hands dirty and dismays supposedly high-minded critics:

PG: 'A lot of people in the world of what some people call serious music or concert music would never write a piece of film music because they would be afraid that their credibility as art composers was compromised. They're bedevilled by notions of this kind which means that they have to teach counterpoint in some university somewhere or they have to cater to a music establishment which has very peculiar ideas about what's relevant in terms of music, and they're being controlled by other people's thoughts about their music. Since what people think about me has very little effect on what I do, I'm very free. Therefore right now there's a play on Broadway, *The Elephant Man*, that has music of mine; there's a film that has music of mine, I have an opera coming out, I did the *Symphony No 6* in January, I do concerts with my ensemble and piano music. There's such a range of activity and I haven't asked anybody's permission to do that, I've just gone and done it myself. If someone doesn't like it, who cares?

'However if you do care, it's a big point, and I think many of my colleagues are blindsighted by these kinds of opinions of other people. If they are worried about that and it's going to bother them, then it does limit what they can do. The idea of going from writing a commercial score to writing an opera which is going to be seen by far fewer people, then to writing a symphony which I'm thinking about, a new symphony, to writing piano music which I'm always doing, the impact that those different kinds of encounters have on the music is extremely stimulating.'

RM: 'I don't know why more composers don't do it that way.'

PG: 'Well they're all teaching counterpoint. We have to understand that first of all there are people who like to teach, so there is that. Second, that profession is a protected environment, they don't have to worry about a pay check. I don't know what will happen next year. I don't know from one year to the next how it's going to work. There's no guarantee. There's no government support or foundation support for this operation whatsoever. It's all done through interacting with the commercial music world on various levels: making records, on the internet, making films, writing operas, there's a whole array of activities which are used to support this.'

RM: 'It's interesting that people 30 or 40 years younger, who are just starting out, are going to look to the way you mix different kinds of work. They're not taking their models from the conservatoire-style composers.'

PG: 'It's becoming easier for them to do that. Whether a piece is art music or is not art music is not important. The real issue is, does the music have any quality? It's very simple. It's a much simpler way of looking at it and in that way you rid yourself of all kinds of ideological and musical–historical notions which are mostly nonsense. You can't pick up a book that was written 30 years ago that makes any sense. Isn't that so? [see PG extract regarding minimalism on p30] In the same way I can say that the younger composers have benefited from the fact that some of the older composers have broken out of the new-music ghetto, and not only have they survived, they're doing quite well. The less they care about the music establishment, the better they do; the less they worry about other people's thoughts about them. However they still have problems.

'Being a young composer today, a man or a woman, it's a very competitive environment. Everybody can make records, everybody can have an internet site, which is good – one of the things that the major labels have been able to do up till now has been to define what is recordable by what they produce and what they put in the stores. Now records simply pour into my home by composers. I cannot keep up with it. There are not enough hours in the day for me to live my life and listen to all the music that comes into my house.

'It's a highly saturated environment and a highly competitive one, and it's quite difficult I think. You put in a lot of time getting to the point where you are asked to do things. I think it's more difficult to be a young writer or composer today than it was 35 years ago. It's a harsher environment. I'm spending time with young composers. I help with a festival every year of about 30 composers. It began as a series at Jonas Mekas' film anthology archive. Also, I'm involved with a place called The Kitchen [one of New York's leading new performance venues: a Center for Video, Music, Dance, Performance, Film and Literature on West 19th Street, between Greenwich Village and Chelsea. Glass's own music is often played at The Kitchen, or used as part of a multi-art presentation, and he has been involved in collaborative work there himself]. We present concerts there so I'm meeting young composers all the time. They're talking to me about what's going on and it's difficult.'

Glass's own collection of responses to the harsher environment, his 'array of activities', is centred on the ninth floor of a small office building on Broadway near Houston Street, a short walk from his East Village house. They share a landing with Bob Marley Music, Inc. On the Glass door, the best known of the nameplates is Looking Glass Studios, a name that appears in the documentation of every Glass recording. The others are Euphorbia Productions and Dunvagen Music Publishing – Dunvagen named after a remote place in Nova Scotia that became Glass's summer retreat over 30 years ago. Inside, the array makes creative and concentrated use of a compact space. A few offices and small meeting rooms open off a corridor, plus there's an archive room into which the main collection of Glass scores and files has recently moved, and the studios are towards the far end.

The main studio is a place full of historical resonance: most of the Glass recordings have been made there and for a visitor it inevitably takes a grip on the imagination. This is where they made that huge sound for *Kundun*. This is where I'm standing now, listening to the mixing of a piece from the 1980s, never released on record before but recorded in a broadcast studio at the time, with a mass of whirling broken chords on voices and synthesizers just like the Philip Glass Ensemble sounded when it toured at the time. It is a surprisingly small and plain room with no acoustic resonance. It seems improbable that big ensembles have recorded there, and indeed the Vienna and Stuttgart orchestras that played the symphonies for CD used their home resources.

The Looking Glass trick is to record section by section. Twelve violins will fit in the room. Then the lower strings come in, then the wind, then the singers. Percussion go in a separate room and the conductor is behind a soundproof partition in the control room. The orchestral film score for *Kundun* was done this way. Then it is over to post-production, assembling the mix from the overlaid parts. Recordings made outside are mixed at the studio. In the control room is a state-of-the-art set of equipment lacking nothing but, evidently, a standard DVD player – Glass was asking for one after an interview session and it turned out that the studio people were in the habit of using computer DVD drives instead. These studios are the domain of resident engineer Kurt Munkacsi, an Ensemble veteran, and Michael Riesman, long-standing keyboard player of the Ensemble and producer or conductor of the recordings. There is a steady turnover of studio apprentices who are learning their trade on some of the best equipment around before they take off to start a career with other studios.

The main triumvirate of Glass, Riesman and Munkacsi has a huge experience of working together and has developed very specific ideas about the art of recording. Munkacsi started out in the early 1970s as the junior engineer in John Lennon's New York studio. When Glass once worked there, Munkacsi was the engineer assigned to the task and got interested in using pop techniques on the music of this oddball classical composer. He helped improve the amplification that Glass used and shortly afterwards joined the Ensemble to work on the sound projection for live performances as well as on recordings. The Looking Glass philosophy is that live and recorded music need completely different approaches. There is no attempt to make the studio recording sound like a live performance. Instead the plan is to unlock the full potential of the technology in support of the music: anathema to many traditionalist musicians, perhaps, but a determinedly creative choice rather than a passive response.

Initially, for example, the Ensemble would play in full in the studio while being multi-tracked on tape, in the belief that this approach best combined the feel of a performance with the ability to adjust the balance and patch up mistakes easily. The team stopped believing this to be the case many years ago. Instead they deliberately construct the recording track by track, overdubbing one at a time even when there is space for everybody to perform at once, because they find they can get a more accurate and exciting performance that way. As the technology has grown more refined, so new possibilities have presented themselves. Even 20 years ago, in the film score for *Koyaanisqatsi*, the sound of orchestral sections was being subtly filled out and almost inaudibly changed by adding synthesizers. Cheating? Not so. It is futile for anybody to be outraged at some imagined dishonesty. This is contemporary music, not GM-free organic farming. The recording is not a distortion of anything, because the music was meant from the start to sound the way it does in the film. That is its natural state.

In music such as the *Koyaanisqatsi* score, which is written for the studio rather than concert performance, Glass was able to start extending the range of what he composed. He could write passages that might be too fast for an instrumental section to play cleanly, knowing that the team could make them performable by a mix of keyboards and the orchestral instruments. The orchestral instruments might play only some of the notes, but the presence of their tone colour and resonance allowed the ear to believe that they were playing all of them. In other places the score for *Koyaanisqatsi* contains passages that would be too dense and complex to work if played live by an orchestra, but which made the desired effect with clarity when selected frequencies were removed from some of the parts in the studio so that the clash of overtones was cut out. The ear accepts the illusion that more is present than really is there. The Looking Glass team has steadily become expert in a kind of practical psychology of listening – knowing what the ear will believe, in more and more circumstances. Good orchestrators have always had a feeling for acoustic effect and illusion, beyond the literal note-playing capabilities of the instruments, and this approach is a conscious extension of their skills. With the rapid development of digital sampling technology, the possibilities have grown ever more subtle.

The Looking Glass Studio produces all Glass's Nonesuch recordings. One of its other activities is to supply material for a new record label based in the building. This is not the first time it has gone down that line:

PG: 'I started Point Music in collaboration with Polygram. It was devoted to new music and we did a lot of new music. We also had to do a certain amount of commercial music, we did some arrangements of rock music as well for orchestra. We did a lot of other composers, Jon Gibson, Gavin Bryars, but I wanted to do a record for Polygram that would boost the sales. [This was the *Low Symphony*.] My arrangement with them was that I would make records of music that I liked that might not sell very well, and I would balance that with records that I also liked that would sell very well. We made records for about ten years, and ended up making about 60 records for that company. Some of them are quite good, about half of them are good in the sense that they are records of music that would not have been recorded had we not done it.

'It was a good project. It stopped when it was bought by the company, by Polygram. They had an option to either buy it or continue it and they decided to buy the company. I'm not part of that company any more. They have the catalogue, and it's no longer in my control any more. We had a ten-year run with them and I think that was fine. I would take a ten-year contract with anyone. You can do a lot in ten years. Don't forget intendants and conductors of operas, they only get five-year contracts. Maybe ten years if it's renewed. And in that period you can do a lot of work. The Stuttgart Opera where Dennis [Russell Davies] was for ten years did a lot of things. He also did a lot of things later with the Vienna Radio Orchestra. Ten years gives you a good range of time to develop ideas, to do cycles of music, to discover composers, to emphasize composers you're interested in.

'We're starting a new record company now, Orange Mountain Music, which is partly based on my archives. We have about 20 titles that have never been released and so we're starting with that. Michael Riesman, a long-time associate of mine, is mixing right now a piece called *The Descent Into The Maelstrom*, based on a poem of Edgar Allen Poe. It was a dance theatre work commissioned by the Australian Dance Theatre at Adelaide in 1989, and we ended up making a very good recording so that they could use it for broadcast. I would like to give the company up to 50 or 60 titles. I would like it to run for about ten years and then someone else might take it on, or we might continue it ourselves. I intend to include other composers. After I've done my first ten records we're going to start bringing in other composers. Right now we're going to use my catalogue as a kind of centre of gravity. We're doing distribution in individual countries as well as on the internet, selling through Amazon. So it's quite a nice project.'

Studio work and thinking about CD releases are afternoon business. The focused working life has a rhythm centred on the most effective use of creative time. That means mornings. When Glass is in New York he starts the day early and turns to the writing first. There may be several new pieces on the go, sometimes with very tight deadlines – especially if he has a commercial commission. There are revisions and retouchings, some urgent again, for music that has to be adjusted while in rehearsal or production. Everything else that he does, and all the office operations, are arranged so that this time is clear. What happens next depends on circumstances but, one way or another, it is generally about the business of music. Meetings, negotiations, interviews, recordings, rehearsals, making plans, checking out written or recorded material...all this is for the later part of the working day. Evenings are personal: family, friends, reading, cooking, music and art events.

Of course rules are made to be bent, and the staff at Dunvagen are likely to tell you that he is due to be coming into the office that day but they don't know exactly when. He may even show up in the morning and drop off some newly written pages. But if an appointment is made, then he will be there. The main alterations in this rhythm are down to touring and out-of-town performances. Because of the sheer quantity of Glass performances around the world and the global spread of premières, he is absent for substantial periods for the Ensemble tours, and he plays recitals. As he told an audience in Los Angeles in 1998 before the première of *Monsters Of Grace*, he makes a point of going back to the same places to develop the audience, and to some extent he sees it as a duty to do this when artistic culture is hemmed in by television culture. He feels he has to keep working at this development task in places where there are all kinds of other shows and distractions. It all takes time too. That makes the protection of the composing time when he is in town doubly important. As a result, he delivers the pieces when they are needed.

It seems to be a general condition of composing that 'writer's block' and late delivery are afflictions of people who have time on their hands. The less work they have on, the less pressure they are under, the more freedom they have to be uncertain about what they have just written, and the worse they suffer. 'I don't have the time,' Glass once replied when he was asked about 'getting stuck'. If you have to get it done tomorrow, because of what has to be done the day after, then you do. Glass is quite confident about taking on projects at short notice in the right circumstances. 'When a film score comes in,' he remarked on appearing in the office suddenly one morning and in the course of apologizing for a postponed interview, 'you have to take it. It pays the rent on this place. The operas don't do that.' This one had appeared ten days earlier and had to be done straight away. It was for Hollywood and that is unusual, only the third time; all the producers normally use career film composers. So the time to do it was made, as he explained. He was wearing his customary expression that combines a frank and open gaze with a slightly puzzled frown. A few minutes later, after several quiet and to-the-point conversations with the associates he needed to see, he was off home again to resume writing.

Workaholic? Glass has too much time for other people and other activities. He has been married four times and has three children. He reads widely and has, for a composer, an unusual interest in the other arts and in the wider world. None of his music is conceived in isolation; most of it has a dramatic, literary, philosophical or visual connection, and the rest is specifically geared to particular conditions of performance. He has his Buddhist practice and his social commitments, whether on the down-to-earth level of working with young composers or by addressing human issues and concerns through the texts and scenarios he chooses. On a personal basis, whatever people think of his music, he seems to be almost universally liked. All these aspects of life are related. The words 'ordinary' and 'ordinariness' crop up in his more reflective interviews: 'There is a way of thinking about ordinary life in a distinctly Buddhist way, and I think that's the real practice.' The building blocks of the music are 'ordinary' accompaniment figures and arpeggios and pulses. But what they turn into is completely personal and, in its reach, apparently universal. 'The impulse that brings us to music', he has said, 'is one of rejoicing.' No workaholic ever said that about their obsession.

Scene 7
Looking Back

For a style as distinctive and influential as Philip Glass's, there is a question that is surprisingly hard to answer. Where did it come from? The subject is hardly one that he has kept quiet about. Far from it, potted biographies in concert programmes have a standard version and Glass has talked freely in interviews. But it is never the full story. Every source seems to tell a different part of it. To get anything like a full view you need to read everything, and even then there is more to ask.

In the standard version, Glass's inspiration came from India. The kick-start was supplied by the rhythmic workings of Indian music. Presented with the challenge of notating North Indian rhythms for Western musicians to play, he quickly noticed that music could be organized in a way that was different from building structures out of harmony and melody. Shortly afterwards he realised that this was a principle he could use for his own composing. As far as it goes, the episode is quite true. The most typical processes in Glass's initial mature phase of composition, repeating and extending rhythmic patterns, crystallized soon after he first encountered the subcontinent's classical music, and he has always said that he found the technique as a direct consequence. This did not, incidentally, mean that he heard Indian music the way it was meant to be heard. As he pointed out in a 1992 interview with *Tricycle* magazine, which was otherwise mainly about Buddhism, 'I thought I was listening to music that was built in an additive way, but it turned out it really wasn't. It is built in a cyclic way. And that turned out to be really useful because the misunderstanding, the use of an additive process, became, in fact, the way I began to write music.'

The context in which he first heard Indian music turns out to be of real significance. This musical encounter happened while he was living in Paris in the mid-1960s. He had gone there to pursue studies of harmony and counterpoint with Nadia Boulanger, one of the great teachers of the 20th century and a magnet to American composers for decades. While he submitted himself to this discipline, he stopped writing his own concert music, which he had been producing steadily throughout his student days. During his second year in Paris, a musician who knew him put him forward for an interesting piece of casual work: transcribing some Indian music for a group of European musicians to play. It was the score for what was to become a cult film, *Chappaqua*, made by the American director Conrad Rooks and released in 1966. This was a semi-autobiographical tale from the hippy generation, featuring Jean-Louis Barrault, William Burroughs and Allen Ginsberg, as well as the author himself in the main role. Rooks's plan had been for the jazz musician Ornette Coleman to provide the film with music. Then he ran into Ravi Shankar when Shankar was passing through Paris. Rooks had got to know him in New York, and the chance meeting prompted him to change his mind about the film score.

The great Indian exponent of the sitar had not yet become a cult figure in hippydom – that began the following year thanks to his appearances at American pop festivals and his friendship with George Harrison. Even afterwards, he often made it clear that while he enjoyed the open minds and free living of this generation, he never cared for drug culture. He was uneasy to find that some film music he had innocently provided in 1965 for Timothy Leary appeared to have become part of a project to glamorize drugs around the university campuses. Now Rooks's film put him back in that world. The film made play with hallucination and drying-out, as well as imaginary scenes about India. Shankar himself has called it 'bizarre', so there is no doubt that he knew what he would be putting his name to this time. But whatever his scruples about the content, he went ahead and accepted the commission. He liked the people involved, and a musical challenge is a musical challenge. Rooks himself became fascinated by India and spent much time there. His second feature film, starring Shashi Kapoor and made in 1972, was of Hermann Hesse's novel *Siddhartha*. In recent years he has lived reclusively in Thailand and has been reported to be writing a book about his life.

Shankar was travelling as usual with the tabla player Alla Rakha, and the idea was to use the two of them plus a small ensemble of Paris-based musicians. But how were they to get the European players to learn the music, players who were used to scores while Shankar had no experience of Western notation? One of them decided that Philip Glass was just the man for the job and asked him along. The intention was that he would learn the music aurally from Shankar and then just write it down for the others to play. Life is rarely so simple, though, and

Glass temporarily got stuck. The problem was in the rhythms. He could not work out how to put them down so that the accents fell in the right place; there seemed to be an extra dimension that he could not fathom. On the other hand he found what Shankar and Alla Rakha were playing and talking about quite fascinating. It was his first real experience of music from outside the European and American traditions. He was particularly impressed with the way that performing and composing in a classical style could be indivisible, rather than existing as two separate functions as they do in most Western music. You did not choose whether to train as a composer or a performer, or how to make time to pursue both studies. You learned at great length through a kind of apprenticeship to a senior musician how to make music, using the skills of memory and imagination and physical technique.

Even before Glass found the rhythms a problem, he was struck by their primacy in the music, more than by the obvious absence of harmonic movement. He got talking with the Indian musicians in some detail. He was impressed by Shankar as a human being, by his warmth and openness and his active interest in discussing musical matters across the board with a puzzled and determined young American. But it was Alla Rakha who helped him reach a solution to his problem, when it dawned on Glass that the rhythmic patterns of Indian music resulted from adding up beats into larger wholes, rather than dividing them into ever smaller fractions (crotchets, quavers, semiquavers) as in Western music.

More than three decades later, Glass spoke at length about what happened before and during the recording of the music for

Chappaqua. The interviewer was his second cousin Ira Glass, a radio talk show host. The two of them barely knew each other. They both came from Baltimore, but Philip had already left to start his university studies in Chicago by the time Ira was born. Now they had been brought together at the Field Museum in Chicago for a public conversation. There was a lot of banter and much family reminiscence, and then Ira asked about Ravi Shankar. Philip took off on an unexpectedly detailed explanation. Extracts are reprinted here courtesy of Philadelphia radio station WHYY, Inc:

PG: 'I went to see Ravi and the session was in three or four days, I said I'm a little worried, could you start showing me how this music works? Then we began talking about music and a lot of other things. And he completely forgot and we never got round to notating it.

'I came the next day and said, "I'd like to start writing the music that we're going to be recording" and he said, "yes, we will do that later. Let's have some tea first and then we can." What he wanted to do was talk about modern music. He was asking me to explain to him how Stockhausen worked and he wanted to know who John Cage was, and I was getting into these impromptu discussions about contemporary music. Meanwhile I was trying to write this music down. Finally, the day of the first session arrived and we hadn't written a note of music. I knew the musicians were going to be there when we got there. I said, we have to start doing this work. What I didn't realise, I discovered it years later, was that when Ravi was working in for example Bombay, this is exactly what he did. He would walk into the studio. The musicians would be sitting there and he hadn't written a note of music, they would wait for him and he would just give it to them on the spot. So he didn't understand what my problem was, that I had to have this music written down but I didn't know how to notate it at all.

'The biggest problem was how to organize the music. We got to the studio two hours early. Then we spent two hours tuning the tambura [this is the usual instrument that provides the drones of North Indian classical music – it has four notes and has to be tuned to the key of performance], which I ended up playing; he spent two hours teaching me how to be the accompanist. Finally the session started and everybody was sitting ready for the music and Ravi. Then they projected the film. He looked at the picture and he began playing the sitar, and I had to write down what he was playing.

'The difficulty was writing it down in a notation that would reflect the rhythmic feeling of what he was playing. To be truthful we solved the problem relatively quickly, but it still took three or four hours. I figured out that there were no bar lines. There weren't any measures, so I got rid of them entirely. There were a string of notes. However, I grouped them and I bracketed them by subgroups of twos and threes and fours, and then I discovered – he never explained this to me – that there was a cycle of beats that kept recurring and that every time I came to the end of the cycle it began again. After that I realised the cycles would be divided into four, four, four, four, or five, five, two, two, two, or three, three, four, three, three. All this would add up to 16. So by the afternoon I realised that the trick of notation was that every line would add up to 16, and that what I had to do was make sure that I organized the groups of notes in such a way that the accents came in the right places.

'Still, it didn't quite work. I would write something down and we would play it and it didn't sound right. I would write it again and it didn't sound right. Alla Rakha kept saying all the notes are the same, all the notes are equal, but I had no idea what he really meant. Finally I realised that it wasn't a question of taking a cycle and dividing it up. It was a question of adding up. The cycle consisted of units that were added on to each other.

'The point was that it was a different way of organizing rhythm. Within a few days of working with Ravi I understood something which I found astonishing, that music could be organized in a completely different way than I had thought. Then I began listening to other music, and I realised that the tradition of Western classical music or popular music was only one way of describing how music can be organized. From that moment on I got interested in music from other parts of the world.'

What Glass does not say is that struggling to come to terms with the nature of Indian music is a common experience, even in India. It takes a different, analytical kind of mind to realise that a general principle about rhythm could be extracted from the experience and applied to other kinds of music. Inventing a new kind of music using the same principle is another thing again. That was the stroke of genius. It did not matter that the principle was not quite what he thought it was, the point was what it then made possible. The episode gave a fresh start to him and a new direction to a whole musical culture.

The element of misunderstanding was quite subtle. He had picked up everything that was going on. But he had the priorities back to front. He thought the fundamental building blocks of the music were the notes, the units that added up, rather than the regular cycles of fixed length within which the units add up. It is easy enough to see why he thought that, because in Indian music you hear only the units. The cycles are not played, they are internally counted by the performers. Cross-rhythms, extended irregular patterns and all the other flights of fantasy have to be devised so that they culminate and come together on the first beat of a new cycle, and sometimes they run through more than one complete cycle before they do come together. Usually the performers will tell their audience in advance how many beats are in the cycle they will use, to make it easier to follow progress from the start. Experienced listeners can work out the length of the cycle for themselves by noticing when the passing events of the music begin and end. They can also see the performers giving cues to one another. But this is not something that a new listener can do straight away; it has to be learnt.

By the time Glass had learnt it, he was already in command of his personal breakthrough and well down the track in writing the precursors of his classic minimalist scores. To an innocent ear there is nothing very Indian at all about Glass's music of the 1960s and 1970s, except for the amount of counting that the players have to do, and the primacy of rhythm. But it is not Indian rhythm. The structures proliferate and extend ever outwards by systematically adding beats to a repeating phrase. The melodic lines are completely Western, using diatonic scales rather than Indian modes, and they are much more repetitive. This is not to say that Glass did not stay interested in Indian music. When Shankar and Alla Rakha went to New York the following year, Glass met up with them and took some tabla lessons, though the musicians then lost touch. Shankar was aware of Glass's subsequent rise to fame. When he learned a few years later that it was as a result of their short encounter that Glass's musical life had been transformed, he was, he said, 'pleasantly surprised'.

As it happened, the impact of Indian culture on Glass's life in broader terms was to be substantial and continuing. Glass travelled to India after he left Paris, which was to be the first of many journeys there, and even on this occasion the focus of his interest shifted to Tibetan Buddhism. Later he sought out dance rather than music. All this has gone towards shaping his life and interests, and sometimes the dramatic or literary content of the work he has chosen to do, whether in *Kundun* or in the texts of *Symphony No 5*. As far as the composing technique is concerned, it is extra-curricular. The experience of Indian music was more in the nature of a trigger that set off the creative explosion, not the start of a continuing relationship. Interrelated cycles of rhythm eventually work their way into his music, but they do so in his own manner and as a development in an already established style. As for the use of repetition on a small scale, that was in the air of creative American music at the time, and it is also more relevant that he spent time in North Africa, where he was fascinated by the repetitive visual patterns of Muslim design and architecture. Glass's second collaboration with Shankar, which was for the album *Passages* in 1989, was certainly the meeting of two very different minds with well known musical personalities of their own: Shankar improvized Indian-style on Glass's themes and Glass composed Western pieces from Shankar's.

What he took from Alla Rakha was, rather, the right discovery at the right time. So why was this the right time? Until then, he had pursued a fairly conventional musical education. It had its quirks and in retrospect they are interesting. In his home town of Baltimore, where he was born in 1937, he learned the flute, played in a local band and joined the school orchestra. The latter used to play for stage shows and operettas. It was his introduction to pit orchestras, and Glass has acknowledged its importance in making him absorb early on how singers worked with players, how themes functioned, what happened in the intervals – all of the basics of musical theatre and opera. But there was an extra dimension at home. Glass's father Ben, a classic first-generation American, started out as a car mechanic, took on mending the car radios when they became a common feature and became so interested in their workings that he opened a radio shop. After a while he heeded somebody's advice and stocked a few records. Gradually the record lines grew and grew until they dominated the shop apart from a bench at the back where radios were still repaired. He kept a close eye on the sales of records, and when there were releases that did not go well he would take copies home to listen to. He wanted to find out what was wrong with them. What he found was that they might be chamber music, or Bartók, or Shostakovich. This was the 1940s and public taste for classical music in Baltimore, as in most other places, was centred on the romantic orchestral composers. Ben Glass had no prior musical knowledge but he learned about music as he went along and became fascinated by what he heard. As time went by he even became something of a fan of the unpopular music, and could be found back in the shop urging customers to sample the joys of the latest Britten issue. This, according to his son, made him something of a shaper of musical taste among the people who used the shop.

While he kept on top of the catalogue at work, the rest of the family had a strange musical diet consisting of what came home. Glass grew up in the presence of specialist, often contemporary, sometimes obscure, usually high-quality, music. As an older boy with a flair for music he put in some time working in the family business and then got to know the range of what was available on record. He was even the classical buyer for a while and was responsible for stocking some 'wrong' records when they came out. Later on he ran a branch in a different area of the city – this was before desegregation – that sold mainly black music. This meant that he knew a wider range of pop than most of his friends. His musical experience had taken on a distinctive twist in the years when everything sticks. Eventually he went on to college and found himself formally studying music that is most listeners' starting point. Before that, as an exceptionally bright student, he was admitted early to university and in 1952 he moved to Chicago with his family's blessing, to read mathematics and philosophy and, by his own account, to take off from time to time and sample the black music scene live – something that only really interested and determined white people did at the time. But he was writing and playing his own music all the time, initially fired up by the contemporary records he had discovered at home. The 19-year-old graduate faced the inevitable, took off to New York and enrolled at the Juilliard School of Music for a full-length course of study, supporting himself with whatever odd jobs came his way.

As Thomas Appleton's 19th-century *bon mot* has it, good Americans, when they die, go to Paris. Glass emerged from the Juilliard and still felt the need of more groundwork in composition. In following the trail of aspiring colleagues across the Atlantic to the lessons of Nadia Boulanger, Glass was statistically putting himself in line for the quiet creative death of an obscure college professorship that was the fate of many of them. Something saved him from that, and it was certainly not just a few days' efforts to get to grips with transcribing Indian rhythm. When he left the Juilliard he was writing music in a conventional symphonic mould, after the models of Roy Harris and William Schuman, and a little more adventurously, Aaron Copland, in the way that was taught there. It included concertos and quartets, and he was able to have the invaluable experience of hearing some of it played by student groups, so that he knew how the sounds in his imagination turned out when he tried to write them down. It gave him all the credentials he could need to support his composing with a teaching position in mid-century America, had he wanted it. He only stopped doing it when he temporarily gave up composing for his two years of counterpoint and harmony with Boulanger. The decision to submit himself to these rigours was naturally born of dissatisfaction; why else endure the hardships of being a student again? But the nature of the dissatisfaction was not precise enough for him to know where the trip would take him. The driving force appears to have been deeper-rooted than a question of technique. And there was another factor: getting involved with a radical theatre company.

While he was in Paris, Glass became part of a radical theatre company along with JoAnne Akalaitis, who was to be his first wife –

she joined him there from the United States. It subsequently set up in New York as the Mabou Mines company, and he kept up his links with it for many years. In Paris the performances were about as fringe as fringe could get, being given on a small scale in English by Americans, and struggled to find an audience. But they were nothing if not pioneering. The company staged plays by the avant-garde of the time, and introduced Glass to an aesthetic that was to affect him crucially. 'These writers,' he recalled in the *Tricycle* interview, referring specifically to Beckett, Brecht and Genet, 'took the subject out of the narrative. They broke the pattern of the reader identifying with the main character.'

This is the stance that in relation to Brecht has been called 'alienation', but however well known the term, it seems misleading especially when there are musical consequences to be considered. The art is not supposed to alienate the reader. It just involves readers in a different way, a more direct way than making them see the drama through the eyes of a person with whom they sympathize. To take the example that will be most familiar to musical readers, *The Threepenny Opera*, the 'Beggar's Opera' story is told in such a way that you judge the characters from their actions rather than putting yourself in their shoes. The question of how to find appropriate music, if it is to be used for the play, may be faced to various extents. It is arguable that, for instance, Kurt Weill in composing for Brecht succeeded too well in a conventional operatic sense, evoking levels of pathos that get you identifying all over again.

Glass had been trying to match the spareness of, say, a Beckett text with music that would have a similar effect. Lighting and text were working closely together in these productions, and the music needed to be with them. The problem was how to organize it so that he did not end up with an apparently random sequence of notes. With only a single line the traditional answer was melody, unaccompanied melody. But the emotional associations of melody would get in the way; they invite listeners to identify with the mood, instead of helping them to observe it. The encounter with Indian music came just as Glass was trying out alternatives. Once he realised that here was an alternative way of organizing music, by rhythm instead of harmony or melody, the next step was to put it into practice. The opportunity came with Beckett's *Play*. The theatre not only gave him the reason for searching, it provided the laboratory for testing the discovery. It also gave him an early experience of musicians resisting what he wanted to do, but he persisted. The timing could not have been better. Not only was he working in the area that was his real passion, he had gotten away from the demands of classical music as he had learnt it up to this point, since he had suspended his conventional creative work while he studied with Boulanger. He could focus undistracted on this after-hours composition.

Knowing this has always made it seem as though there was a discovery waiting to happen, to suit the needs of the theatre work, and that what Glass initially took from Indian music was not so much a fresh start for its own sake as the solution to a specific practical problem he had:

PG: 'That was happening at the same time. I began working in theatre when I was 20. We founded this theatre when I was 26 so I'd already been doing theatre pieces and dance pieces and even some small film pieces, but the commitment to working with that theatre generated a continuous flow of music. There was one piece after another and it went on for 15 years. I went on for quite a long time working with them later, right into the early 90s.

'The thing about the theatre is that it usually creates unique demands on a composer. There are dramatic situations that can't be accounted for in the techniques that you have. It's for that reason that the theatre has always been a breeding ground for new ideas in music, whether it was Monteverdi or Verdi or Stravinsky. When you're working with theatre you're always dealing with unexpected things and it usually is an occasion to develop techniques. That technique becomes what you end up working with, and that is very much what happened. First with the Mabou Mines, I was able to use a lot of these new ideas with that company, and then with *Einstein On The Beach* a further extension of those ideas. I think it's fair to say that without the occasion of these theatre pieces, the development of the language wouldn't have happened so rapidly, because there was a constant demand for new work and new forms. So I began to implement innovations in the musical language, and it happened to be the time I was working with Ravi, so they became the materials that I was working with and the theatre became the opportunity to try them out. They really did work hand in hand.'

Looking back in May 2002, Glass confirms that when he went to Paris to study with Nadia Boulanger, it was not to try and find a new language but to develop his technique:

PG: 'It was for technical reasons. I felt that the conservatory training I had had been a little lax. It's supposedly the best school in the country, the Juilliard, but my impression was that their strategy was to have very difficult entrance exams so that the best students came there, and very easy graduation exams. The students were expected through their talent and the environment they were working in, with so many other talented people, to develop, and they kind of left them alone. And it really did work that way. There were so many gifted student musicians around, and the atmosphere was so conducive to working, that at the end of the five years that I was there it seemed to me that I had learnt the technical language on the job, so to speak. I didn't really have an overview on top of this and it was for that reason that I went to study with Boulanger. She provided exactly what I was looking for, several years of harmony and counterpoint and analysis but everything from a completely clear perspective. I was really thinking of polishing and refining, and not just that but rethinking my whole technical language in a coherent way. She did do that, that was her forte.'

RM: 'So what actually happened was something that developed while you were in Paris, not the reason you went there in the first place.'

PG: 'That's right. Admittedly I met Ravi there, if I had been in New York I wouldn't have met him. I think eventually I would have encountered world music because in the mid- to late 60s it was so much a thing that was about to happen. I was a little bit ahead of it because meeting him in 1965 gave me a bit of an edge. Also meeting someone of his accomplishments and his seriousness of purpose put it into a much more serious context than if I had just listened to some world music records in New York and then tried to imitate them, without any contact with people who were masters of that tradition. It was a tremendous help meeting them and in fact studying with Alla Rakha for a while, back in New York when they turned up in 1967 – Ravi was a visiting professor at the City College of New York and Alla Rakha was here.'

It is worth clearing up another misunderstanding, about Glass's musical relationship with Africa. Put simply, there is none. You can sometimes read that there is, and even that musical research was his reason for going to North Africa, but neither was the case. The only intentional contact had come back in New York, and it was interesting rather than creatively productive:

PG: 'I was travelling in North Africa, I did listen to music while I was there but that wasn't the primary reason. I had been involved with a workshop at Columbia University that was being given in African music, in 1967 or 1968, and a number of us went to those. Anyone could go to those, you didn't have to be a student at Columbia. There was an African master drummer who was maybe studying economics here, but not music, and he began giving classes in African music – it wasn't teaching but he gave us an opportunity. Steve Reich was there as well as Jon Gibson, also a composer who plays with me, so we had an additional exposure to another tradition which though it works in terms of cyclic music works in a very different way. African music can be polymetric but it doesn't necessarily add up to one overriding cycle, it's done in layers. Indian music is also organized in layers or cycles but there's always a larger rhythmic cycle that they add up to. In that way African music is more similar to Balinese and Javanese music, but I'm not really expert in that at all. I heard some of that music but I did not begin playing in one of those Balinese bands that were around at that time.'

Glass has always insisted on the importance of his two years' study with Nadia Boulanger. It sounds paradoxical, but the story of his music finding its language is one of casting off unwanted baggage. First, he tried the way that in the 1950s was considered most advanced: serial composition in the style of Schoenberg and his followers, which was catching on rapidly in Europe and in a few pockets of American academia. He had heard the recordings in his father's shop. But he worked his way out of it before he went to the Juilliard. There was plenty of it about in Paris when he went there, since it was the heyday of Pierre Boulez and his fellow graduates from another dominant force in composition teaching, Olivier Messiaen. By this time it no longer even interested him, and he only showed up at the city's avant-garde concerts when there was something else on the programme to draw him, particularly an adventurous American composer such as Morton Feldman or Earle Brown. He had learnt to write in the mainstream American tradition taught at colleges all over the continent, often by Boulanger pupils. Going to Paris was a natural continuation. Yet, by the time he left, having had enough of study, he had performed another rejection act and abandoned the tradition he was apparently destined for. He did this, but at the same time he was generous in praise of the teaching that was supposed to prepare him for it, and he continues to be so.

The point about Boulanger's lessons is that they were radical in the extreme. They stripped Western music right down to its elements of melody, counterpoint, harmony and notation. A rock-solid technique had to begin from scratch. Everything in music had to happen for a reason, and the musician had to be conscious of it. Only when the technique had been painstakingly built up could there be any question of personal style. Yet the two were inescapably bound together. As Glass puts it, style is a special case of technique, and he has often talked about reaching a breakthrough point when he understood how Boulanger was teaching the relationship between them. For on a subtle level she was teaching the classical style as it established itself in the time of Mozart and Beethoven. She succeeded, too. Boulanger was a key figure in establishing the 20th-century movement known as Neo-Classicism, which until at least the middle of the century was more influential on composers than the serial methods. She professed tradition, but she did so on such a fundamental level that her teaching became a force for innovation as well as conservation. It all depended on the vision of her students.

One of her tactics was to present a class with one written line of music and, over perhaps a four-hour period, draw out of them not just a harmonization of it but the 'right' one. For it would turn out that she had chosen, say, one of the inner parts of a chamber work by Beethoven. The class had been steered towards a solution that did not just follow the classical rules, but made the same choices as the original composer. It would have been a lot quicker if the students had guessed the work, but she was cunning enough to find musical lines that were hard to identify out of context. Glass has recalled a confrontation with Boulanger over this method, which finally opened his eyes to the full content of her teaching. He delivered his harmony exercise to her and waited as she read it. One of the chords, she decided, was wrong. By this time Glass was thoroughly on top of his craft and came back to her with confidence: no, it's right, it obeys the rules. It's still wrong, she insisted. The argument continued, and finally she showed him why. You can harmonize this passage in several different ways, all technically correct in classical terms. Only one of them, however, was the way Mozart used to choose when he was composing a similar passage. She played him several examples to prove the point. So the chord was right, and it was also wrong. It depended on what you meant to do.

For Glass, this exchange made him understand, as though for the first time, the full relationship between technique and style. Each style – Mozart's, Beethoven's, Rachmaninov's – may be technically correct. Each will deal with musical situations in a different way, but each composer will tend to make the same choice every time he faces the same situation. Style is a special case of technique because it depends on choices made using a correct technique. This is how we recognize the composer from the sound of the music. It also means that a clear style is not possible without a correct technique; the choices will not be fully informed ones and might just as well be random. At this point, realising that he had acquired the technique he needed and that he had to find his style elsewhere, he got 'sick of school' and his formal education came to an end. When he came to develop his own style, he could build it up with confidence because he knew exactly what he was doing with the elements. It was a stripped-down style to start with, and without knowing it he had given himself the best possible preparation for it.

What is more, it developed hand in hand with his practice of Tibetan Buddhism. As Glass put it in the *Tricycle* interview, the three fundamentals of Boulanger's teaching were 'paying attention, making an effort, and always the basics'. She was capable of complete focus and concentration on the essential issues, and expected the same of her students. That is why she was such a demanding teacher. Her approach was vocational to a degree of severity that was tantamount to monastic training. The parallel goes further because by apparent coincidence, and without being aware of it, she had hit on a set of disciplines recalling the three Buddhist practices that the Dalai Lama summarizes in his 2002 book, *How To Practise*, as morality, concentrated meditation and wisdom.

This is not Glass's observation and he would not have put it that way, but being led towards Buddhism was another consequence of his interest in India and Indian culture. On his early travels to the subcontinent he went, like many Western visitors, to the home of the Tibetan government in exile with its concentration of Buddhist monasteries, in the Himalayan foothills between Dharamsala and Macleod Ganj. Here he first heard the chanting and the instruments that all visitors hear, the same ones that he was to use in the score for *Kundun*. Over the intervening years he has met the Dalai Lama several times and has given performances as a prelude to the Lama's public appearances in New York. Glass gets annoyed if he is called a Buddhist composer, and even more if it is suggested that his music is designed for meditating. (There is nothing to stop you meditating to it if you want, but his attitude is the same as that of any other composer, that his music is designed for listening.) The interviews for the present book did not cover Buddhism, and the subject has been kept until the end. It is part of his life, not of his music. It is in the way he works, not the work itself. Even in *Kundun*, the Buddhist content is in the lives of the people it is about. The film tells a story, and the music sounds like Glass's music. It does what Glass chooses from the techniques at his disposal. *Kundun* happens to be about something he is personally involved with, and somebody he personally knows. But that is as far as it goes.

Rather, it is that the discipline and focus of Glass's composing practice are similar to the discipline and focus of Buddhist practice. They were even acquired in similar ways. You could say that the practice of music, as taught by Boulanger, is like a special case of the practice of living, as taught by Buddhists. You can go a little further as an observer, and notice that the carefully controlled working life and the carefully controlled music appear to have in common the qualities of self-awareness and practised command of the raw materials. But all good music is based on knowledge and technical confidence, and it is not usually called Buddhist. So there is an end to the matter.

What remains is to close the circle up to the emergence of Glass the theatre and opera composer that he became a quarter of a century ago. As far as writing about him is concerned it is well trodden ground, already part of the history of music even as it is taught in colleges now. So this is the briefest of conclusions. Once he had finished studying with Nadia Boulanger, theatre continued to lead the way. Glass and

Akalaitis had taken time out while they were in Europe to visit other dramatic centres, including London and Berlin. They spent more than a week watching productions by the Berliner Ensemble, Brecht's old company, in what was then East Berlin. All this experience went into the continuing work, but the company members soon moved to New York when they accepted that there was not enough of an audience for English-language work in Paris, and there they continued to develop their ideas, including musical ideas. There too, Glass gradually assembled around him a nucleus of musicians who could handle the scores he was writing. The music used rhythm as its main element of change. It was almost devoid of harmony and used a minimum of melodic material, just enough notes to create the short phrases that could repeat, extend and proliferate into substantial forms. It needed more than instrumental skill, it came to depend on stamina and an ability to hold together fast, gradually changing patterns. The Philip Glass Ensemble began to give performances of its own, in studios and galleries and lofts. As the ensemble gelled, Glass was able to write more ambitiously for it and the repertoire that became known as the definitive embodiment of minimalism in music took shape.

Doubtless because of the parallel with minimal painting, New Yorkers in the visual arts were quicker on the uptake in understanding the music than the mainstream musical community. Much of the time in the late 1960s and early 1970s, the ensemble's performances took place in association with temporary exhibitions at art museums. Between 1972 and 1974 Glass had a studio in Bleecker Street, Greenwich Village, where he would give few concerts to an audience of up to 200, attracted by word of mouth – no advertising, partly because of the space limitations. One quirky event at this time took place on the initiative of the Institute for Art and Urban Resources, a mould-breaking arts organization run by the redoubtable Alanna Heiss. It was a concert under Brooklyn Bridge. Literally under: the musicians set up on the Brooklyn side of the river near one of the main pillars. The ensemble was to play *Music In Similar Motion* and *Music In Fifths*. The concert was meant to start after a dinner but was delayed by two hours because it was raining and there were problems with the outdoor electric current supply. This meant that most of the audience, and reportedly some of the performers, got thoroughly drunk while they were waiting. Glass recalled later that the sound was very good because the bridge worked like a natural resonating chamber.

Meanwhile the music was not standing still. It reached out to definitive lengths in *Music In Twelve Parts*, with its vast cycles of rhythm fixed by superimposed patterns of different lengths, which would eventually reach their starting points simultaneously. It began to acquire harmony. And it attracted the interest of an artist who was building unique bridges between the visual and performing arts, as though he were discovering the first principles of opera afresh with only the music missing. The two men just had to collaborate. Working with Robert Wilson on *Einstein On The Beach*, the last element fell into place. It was the last act of Philip Glass the figure from music history, the first of Philip Glass now.

List Of Works

The following includes major compositions and collaborations since 1966, insofar as they are acknowledged by Glass's publishing company. Arrangements and extracts from larger works, such as orchestral items from operas, are not listed separately. For concert works involving orchestras see 'For Chamber Orchestras', 'For Orchestra And Soloists' and 'For Orchestra And Voices' as well as 'Orchestral Works'. Note that student pieces are not included. Other works, such as *String Quartet No 1*, have been withdrawn. For the most recent information, contact Dunvagen Music Publishing Inc, 632 Broadway, New York, NY 10012, USA (tel 212-979 2080, fax 212-473 2842), or visit www.philipglass.com

STAGE WORKS

Einstein on the Beach (1976)
A Madrigal Opera (1980)
Satyagraha (1980)
The Photographer (1982)
Akhnaten (1983)
The CIVIL Wars: a tree is best measured when it is down.
    Act V – Rome section (1984)

The Juniper Tree (1985)
A Descent Into The Maelstrom (1986)
The Fall Of The House of Usher (1988)
1000 Airplanes On The Roof (1988)
The Making Of The Representative For Planet Eight (1988)
Hydrogen Jukebox (1990)
White Raven (1991)
The Voyage (1992)
Orphee (1993)
La Belle Et La Bête (1994)
Les Enfants Terribles (1996)
Monsters Of Grace (1997)
The Marriages Between Zones Three, Four And Five (1997)
In The Penal Colony (2000)
The Elephant Man (2002)
Galileo Galilei (2002)

ORCHESTRAL WORKS

The Olympian: official music of the 23rd Olympic Games (1984)
The Light (1987)
The Canyon (1988)
Concerto Grosso (1992)
Low Symphony [No 1] (1992)
Symphony No 2 (1994)
Heroes Symphony [No 4] (1996)
Days And Nights In Rocinha (1997)
Psalm 126 (1998)
DRA Fanfare (1999)
Dancissimo (2001)

FOR CHAMBER ORCHESTRAS

Company (1983)
Phaedra (1986)

In The Upper Room (1986)
Passages (1990)
Symphony No 3 (1995)
Songs Of Milarepa (1997)

FOR ORCHESTRA AND SOLOISTS

Violin Concerto (1987)
Echorus (1995)
Concerto For Saxophone Quartet And Orchestra (1995)
Concerto Fantasy For Two Timpanists And Orchestra (2000)
Tirol Concerto For Piano And Orchestra (2000)
Cello Concerto (2001)
Concerto For Harpsichord And Orchestra (2002)

FOR ORCHESTRA AND VOICES

Itaipu (1989)
Symphony No 5: Requiem, Bardo, Nirmanakaya (1999)
Symphony No 6 (Plutonian Ode) (2002)

CHORAL WORKS

Another Look at Harmony – Part IV (1975)
Three Songs For Chorus a capella (1984)

CHAMBER MUSIC

Head On (1967)
Piece In The Shape Of A Square (1967)
1 + 1 (1968)
Gradus (1968)
Strung Out (1969)
Another Look At Harmony – Part III (1975)
Facades (1981)
Glassworks (1981)
String Quartet No 2, 'Company' (1983)

Prelude to Endgame (1984)
String Quartet No 3, 'Mishima' (1985)
Arabesque in memoriam (1988)
String Quartet No 4, 'Buczak' (1989)
France (1991)
String Quartet No 5 (1991)
Melodies For Saxophone (1995)
Aguas da Amazonia (1999)
Voices For Organ, Didgeridoo
    And Narrator (2001)

FOR ORGAN

Music In Contrary Motion (1969)
Dance No 2 (1978)
Dance No 4 (1979)

FOR PIANO

In Again Out Again (1968)
Two Pages (1968)
Modern Love Waltz (1978)
Mad Rush (1979)
Metamorphosis (1988)
Wichita Vortex Sutra (1988)
Now, So Long After That Time (1994)
Joyful Moment (1998)

SONGS

Hebeve Song (1983)
Songs From Liquid Days (1986)
Planctus (1997)

MINIMALIST ENSEMBLE WORKS

Music In Similar Motion (1969)

Music In Fifths (1969)
Music With Changing Parts (1970)
600 Lines
How Now
Music In Eight Parts (all early 1970s)
Music In Twelve Parts (1974)

FILM MUSIC

North Star (1977)
Koyaanisqatsi (1982)
Mishima (1984)
Hamburger Hill (1987)
Powaqqatsi (1987)
The Thin Blue Line (1988)
Mindwalk (1990)
Candyman (1992)
Compassion In Exile (1992)
Anima Mundi (1992)
A Brief History Of Time (1992)
Candyman II (1995)
Jenipapo (1995)
The Secret Agent (1996)
Bent (1997)
Kundun (1997)
The Truman Show (1998)
Dracula (1998)
Man in the Bath (2001)
Diaspora (2001)
Naqoyqatsi (2002)
The Hours (2002)
The McNamara Project (tba)

Index

and *Symphony No 3* 87
and *Symphony No 5* 98
and *Symphony No 6* 100
and *Tirol Concerto* 117,
118, 119, 122
and violin concerto 124
*The Descent Into The
Maelstrom* 156
Dohnanyi, Christoph von 46,
71
Dortmund 110
dramatic themes, stage works
131
Dunvagen Music Publishing
151

Einstein, Albert 49, 52, 131–2
Einstein On The Beach 15,
33–4, 35–6, 147, 183
influences on 174
not seen in Britain 56
as portrait opera 39
works following 69
Elephant Man, The 20, 149
Les Enfants Terrible 134, 136
English National Opera 38,
134–5
Eno, Brian 90
Low 77, 79, 80, 81
Euphorbia Productions 151
Europe 91
postwar arts funding 63–7
exploration, as dramatic
theme 131, 132

Fall Of The House Of Usher
136
Feldman, Morton 177
Festival Klangspuren 117
film 69
PG on 136–7
film scores 16, 136–43, 158
attitude towards 148
listening to 22–3
Finkel, Ian 114, 116
Flanigan, Lauren 101
focus, artistic 146

Galileo 49–50, 131–2
PG on 50–4
Galileo Galilei 14–15, 20, 38,
49–55, 130
Gandhi 133
Genet, Jean 172
Gibson, Jon 155, 176
Ginsberg, Allen 99–101, 106,
161
Glass, Ben 105, 106, 147,
169–70
Glass, Ira 163–64
Glass, Philip 169
early life 147
music's elements 27
as pianist 119
preconceptions regarding

music by 23–4
and work 144–5
working method 144–59
daily routine 156–7
delivery 157–8
PG on 144
Glassworks 10–11
Gorecki, Henryk 67
Gramophone review,
Symphony No 5 44–5
Greek myth 53
Griffiths, Paul 99
ground bass (see *chaconne*)

Haas, Jonathan 74, 112,
113–14
Hare, David 140
harmony 35–6
harpsichord concerto 20, 128
Harris, Roy 171
Harrison, George 162
Hawking, Stephen 49, 52, 132
Heiss, Alanna 183
Heroes 90–3
Heroes Symphony 8
Hesse, Hermann 162
Heyworth, Peter 12
Hollywood 136–7, 140
Horner, James, PG on 137
Hours, The 16, 20, 140
Houston 134
Hughes, Robert 147–8
Hwang, David Henry 132
Hydrogen Jukebox 100, 131

Impressions Of Tirol 119
Indian music, influence 27,
160–1, 166–8
influences 146–7
inspiration, sources 160–1
Institute for Art and Urban
Resouces 183
instrumental music 43–4, 126–7
Itaipu 71

Jalal-ud-din Rumi 135
Julliard School of Music 147,
170, 175
Junge Deutsche
Kammerphilharmonie 79

Kapoor, Shashi 162
Kidman, Nicole 140, 141
Kiel 134
King, Martin Luther 133
Kitchen, The 151
Koyaanisqatsi 16, 17, 40–1,
140
PG on 136
place in dramatic output
137, 138, 139
recording 154
Kozinn, Allan 99
Kronos Quartet 8, 13, 69
Kundun 16, 140, 142, 152, 168

PG on 136
and Tibetan Buddhism 180,
181
languages, and *Symphony No
5* 95
Leary, Timothy 162
Leibowitz, Rene 62
Lennon, John 153
Lessing, Doris 134, 135
Light, The 46–7, 71, 80, 126,
132
Lisbon 133
listening skills 22–47
Liverpool 110
Lloyd Webber, Julian 122
London 11, 80, 135–6
Barbican Centre 8, 38–9
English National Opera 8,
38, 134–5
Long Yu 122
Looking Glass Studios 151,
152, 153, 154, 155
Los Angeles 137
Low, and *Low Symphony*
77–8
Low Symphony 8, 91, 155
features 81–83
genesis 76, 77–81
reaction to 80
symphonic language 83–5

Ma, Yo Yo 140
Mabou Mines company 172,
174
Maderna, Bruno 62
Mahler, Gustav 84
*Making Of The
Representative Of Planet
Eight* 134
*Marriages Between Zones
Three, Four And Five* 134
Maxwell Davies, Peter 10, 56,
58, 85
melody, after *Einstein On The
Beach* 42–3
Messaien, Olivier 59–60, 62,
177
Metropolitan Opera 34, 132
Michelson, Albert 49
Michelson-Morley experiment
46
millennium, amd *Symphony
No 5* 93
minimalism 44, 67, 144–5
minimalist period, features 28
Mishima 141–2
PG on 136
Mishima, Yukio 142
Monsters of Grace 38, 135–6
Moore, Julianne 140
Morley, Edward 49
Morton, James Parks 94
Munkacsi, Kurt 152–3
music, diversification in late
20th century 67–8